IN HIS IMAGE

REDISCOVERING WHO WE ARE

First Published in Great Britain in 2022

Copyright © Mark Russell

The right of Mark Russell to be identified as the author of this work has been asserted by him in accordance with the Copyright, Designs and Patents Act 1988.

All rights reserved. No part of this publication may be reproduced, stored in a retrieval system, or transmitted in any form or by any means, electronic or mechanical, including photocopy, recording, without the prior written permission of the publisher, nor be otherwise circulated in any form of binding or cover other than that in which it is published and without a similar condition being imposed on a subsequent purchaser.

Unless otherwise stated Scriptures are taken from the Holy Bible, New International Version copyright © 1973, 1978, 1984 by International Bible Society. Used by permission of Zondervan Bible Publishers.

All rights reserved.

Scripture quotations from The ESV® Bible (The Holy Bible, English Standard Version®), copyright © 2001 by Crossway, a publishing ministry of Good News Publishers. Used by permission. All rights reserved.

Scripture quotations marked TPT are from The Passion Translation®. Copyright © 2017, 2018 by BroadStreet Publishing® Group, LLC. Used by permission. All rights reserved. ThePassionTranslation.com.

Scripture quotations from The Authorized (King James) Version. Rights in the Authorized Version in the United Kingdom are vested in the Crown. Reproduced by permission of the Crown's patentee, Cambridge University Press.

Scriptures marked NKJV are taken from the NEW KING JAMES VERSION (NKJV): Scripture taken from the NEW KING JAMES VERSION®. Copyright© 1982 by Thomas Nelson, Inc. Used by permission. All rights reserved.

All emphasis within Scripture quotations is the author's own. Please note that the name satan and related names are not capitalised. This has been the author's choice however the author recognises that it is grammatically incorrect.

ISBN: 978-1-8380446-6-4

Published by Alan Searle Media in the United Kingdom for worldwide distribution, to glorify Christ through creative writing and truthful testimony. Online at http://alansearle.media

Cover design by Lawson Design

Acknowledgements

This book would not have been possible without the support and belief of my beautiful wife, Laura, who has helped greatly with the editing process.

I want to thank my friend Amba Keeble, my sister Cheryl Russell and mother-in-law, Sue Adlard, for your proof reading and excellent suggestions.

I also want to thank my friend and pastor, Vince Turner, for your theological input and words of encouragements.

Finally, I dedicate this book to Father God, without You this book would never have been written. Take my words and use them for Your glory.

Contents

Foreword 1

Introduction 5

My Journey into the Father's Heart 12

Identity 30

Forgiven 53

Made in the Image of God 69

Co-heirs with Christ 85

Adopted as Sons 105

Intimacy 118

Inheritance 140

Chosen 161

The Apple of His Eye 176

Royalty 191

Epilogue 206

About the Author 210

Foreword

In recent years much has been preached and written about who we are in Christ, our identity, our royalty in the Kingdom, our adoption, our inheritance. It has, and continues to be essential. For generations the people of God have lived as though their sin was more powerful than God's grace. While we would never say it out loud – that is how we have lived. False humility & a religious spirit have shut us down, held us down and put us down. (I leave you to find the pages where Mark tackles the "unforgiveable sin").

Much of this teaching has centred around those famous verses in Matthew 22:

> *"One of them, a lawyer, an expert in the law, tested Him with this question: "Teacher, which is the great commandment in the Law?" Jesus replied: "Love the Lord your God with all your heart and with all your soul and with all your mind." This is the first and greatest commandment. And the second is like it: 'Love your neighbour as yourself.' All the Law and the Prophets hang on these two commandments."*

We have been told, rightly so, that this command requires us to love our neighbour as ourselves. Implicit in this is the command to love ourselves – we should love what & who God loves – and God loves us. If however we stop at those commandments we fall short of the new covenant. Jesus was answering the question about commandments "under the law". These were old covenant commandments and we are no longer "under the law". If we stop at this point we end up with a self-centred, me first, spiritual version of the world's "because you're worth it" mentality. If we stop there, Matt Redman's song lyrics "it's all about you Jesus" become "it's all about me".

So, if that is the old covenant commandment, what is the new covenant commandment – especially as the standards of the new covenant are always higher than the standards of the old covenant?

Jesus tells us in John 13 "a new commandment I give unto you that you love one another as I have loved you." It is a new commandment, because it replaces the old commandment. No longer do we get off with loving people like we love ourselves – now we get to love people like Jesus loves them.

In his book, Mark takes us on his personal journey not just into teaching theology about a subject but into his own journey of revelation. Mark's personal journey is appropriately journaled here to give his teaching a heart and a soul as well as a mind. How he came to a place where all these wonderful truths were to be experienced, to "taste and see that the Lord is good".

Mark's extensive use of scripture (don't skip over those verses as you read this book) will give you a reason for the hope that is within you, a foundation that will survive the storm that challenges re-discovered truth. It is worth remembering that the Truth doesn't set you free – it is the <u>Truth you know</u> that set's you free and ultimately the Truth is a Person. Mark is widely read, which with his use of scripture avoids the trap of getting stuck in a spiritual "How to improve your self-esteem" book.

The people of God are re-discovering just how great is His love for mankind and how powerful the destiny and how great the inheritance He has for His children. While God could perfectly achieve all things, He intentionally chooses to partner with imperfect people – God who is perfect is not a perfectionist. Amazingly, Jesus tells His disciples that we would do greater miracles than His disciples saw Him perform.

"Creation groans for the sons of God to be revealed" – enough hiding. Time to see ourselves and others as God sees us and then for creation to feel the benefit of His kingdom being "at hand".

David and Christine West
Directors of Bethel Sozo UK

Mark Russell

Introduction

My hope is that through reading this book God will bring you into a deeper and greater revelation of what it means to be made in His image. Much has been written in recent years about this topic and I believe it is something the Father, in this season, wants His children to gain a deeper revelation of. Therefore I believe this teaching is something that people are receiving in a much greater way than before.

Those of us who have been in church for any length of time may know that we are made in His image and are familiar with Bible verses such as:

"So God created man in His own image, in the image of God He created them; male and female He created them."

Genesis 1:27

In the past when I read or quoted this passage for me it was a piece of knowledge or a fact that I knew. However, at that time

I had not yet experienced a heart revelation about what this really meant.

Father God first spoke to me in early 2015 about putting pen to paper and to begin to share what He had been revealing to me about what it really means to be in His image. Little did I know that when Father spoke this I had been believing a lie; the lie that I was not capable nor had the skills or abilities to write such a book. I have read some excellent books by much more 'qualified' people, world renowned authors and church leaders who are respected both for their Bible knowledge and their own experiences. Father began to show me that because I am made in His image, then I do have the skills and abilities to write such a book. He showed me that the very book He was asking me to write was ironically the very reason I did not think I was able to do it. Father showed me that He is not looking for a polished theological textbook, nor in fact another reworking of what has been written by others; He was simply looking for my obedience. He was looking for me to understand who I am in Him and that because I have been created in His image I do have the ability to complete the task.

Being made in the image of God is one of the most foundational revelations for Christians. I firmly believe that being created in the image of God and all that it entails is one of the most important subjects the Church should be teaching about and living out.

I believe that when we truly understand who we are in Him, who He really is to us, and what He really thinks of us, our lives will be transformed. When our understanding of who we are comes in line with what Father thinks of us, we will never be the same again.

The more I delve deeper into Father and He renews my thinking and the more I allow His truth to dwell in my spirit, the more I realise that there is so much more to explore and to learn!

As I have gained a deeper understanding and revelation of what it means to be created in His image, I have found myself asking what is there that we cannot accomplish when we are in partnership with Him? I believe there is a strong desire in Father to reveal the truth to us in order that we are no longer held back by our fears or perceived failings. It is the tactic of the devil to shield the truth of who we are from us. He wants us to have a false impression that being made in His image are just words and that in reality it does not mean anything. I believe that if we continue to partner with this lie then we will not be able to experience the fullness of what it really means to be made in the image of God. We will not be able to grasp how much more there is to us than what we see and that there is much more for us to experience than what we have thus far in our lives. I believe that because of this lie and tactic of satan, we have not been able to enter completely into the fullness of who we are in Him and we have not been able to experience the full inheritance that Father has for us.

The Bible says in John:

"The thief comes only to steal, kill and destroy; I have come that you may have life, and have it to the full."

John 10:10

The enemy has been hiding the truth from us in order to steal the very life that Jesus came to give us. By listening to this lie we have not fully understood the great love the Father has for us and we have not experienced the fullness of life He bought for us at the Cross. The fullness of life talked about here is abundance of joy and of strength of mind, body and soul. I believe once we appreciate the truth of this love and the depth of love He has for each of us, then this will lead us to a greater understanding of our identity and the intimacy we can have with Him, which in turn leads to a deeper understanding of what it means to be in His image. The journey is one that starts by understanding His love first. We cannot know who we are until first we fully understand who we belong to. It is like looking at a map; it is only when we are on the journey that the map is much more helpful to us.

For far too long the devil has been doing what he does best, deceiving and lying and at times without any fight from us. But now is the time for us, the Church, to rise up and stand in the truth and in victory declare who we are and to fight back against the schemes of the enemy. Let us make every effort to understand and experience who we are, so that we are better able to resist any advance from the enemy. Jesus gave His life in full that we might receive and experience life to the fullest. He gave His life that we might receive life.

Paul writes in Ephesians:

*"And I pray that you, being **rooted** and **established** in love, may have power, together with all the saints, to grasp how wide and long and high and deep is the love of Christ, and to know this love that surpasses knowledge – that you may be **filled** to the **measure** of all the **fullness** of God."*

Ephesians 3:18-19 (emphasis added)

It is time that we become rooted to the very core of our being, in revelation and experience of what it really means for us to be made in His image. As we become rooted in this truth of who we are and all of the wonderful implications of that then we become established in His love, it becomes a permanent feature in our hearts. Why? What is the purpose of this? That we may be "filled to the measure of all the fullness of God." With God there are no half measures, He never does anything that is not complete. The only measure there is with God is fullness. I believe our capacity to experience Him and grow in understanding of who He is can increase, but the measure we have today from Him is always to that same fullness. In other words He always gives according to our ability to receive. As we begin to move deeper into the revelation of who we are, then our capability to experience Him and receive greater revelation will increase. Consider a half pint glass of water which is full, it cannot hold any more. However, a pint glass of water with only half a pint of water is not full, there is more capacity to hold water. As we grow in our understanding and revelation of who we are, it is like we are growing in size from a half pint to a full pint, as we do that we have more room for the water to fill us. We can never out receive from God. In other words, the amount we can receive is always smaller than His ability to give. He will never give us less of Him than we are able to experience. Therefore our measure today should not be our measure tomorrow of the fullness of who He is.

I pray that as you read through the pages of this book your heart will be stirred, your ability to receive the fullness of God will increase and your understanding of who you are will grow. I pray also that you grow in the revelation that Father is always good and loving and what that really means for you; that when this is applied in your life it will cause you to grow into who He has designed you to be.

At the time Father asked me to write this book I experienced a series of pictures and visions from Him. One was of a suit of armour. As I looked I realised this suit of armour was huge; it was like it was made for a giant. I continued to watch and suddenly I was transported into this armour; it became very apparent that this was for me. However, although I was stood in it, it was difficult to say I was wearing it because the armour, though it was mine, did not fit. Father showed me that as I continue on this journey of revelation of who I am and what it means to be in His image, then I would grow into it. I believe this is a picture for us all. No matter where we are on the journey of revelation and understanding of what it means to be created in His image, there is always greater revelation to grow into and therefore our capacity is always increasing.

Prayer:

At the end of each chapter I will be writing a short prayer asking God to show us more of who we are in relation to each of the subjects covered within that chapter.

> *Father I pray that as I read this book you will reveal to me the truth of what it means to be made in Your image. Jesus I thank you that You died for me because You loved me, but that was not the end of the transaction. You want me to have life and have it to the full. Father, would you increase my capacity and my measure so that I might be able to experience and move in the truth of who I am. Amen.*

My Journey into the Father's Heart

I want to spend some time sharing with you my story and journey into greater revelation of the Father's heart, before we unpack and consider the meaning of being in His image and what that means for us today. I will also use the term Father, referring to Father God. In chapter 6 'Co-heirs with Christ' I will expand on this and explain some of the difficulties we often have with the idea of calling God a Father.

For me it has been a process over a period of time and I am still on this journey.

I gave my life to Jesus in 1988, I remember it like it was yesterday but as I have discovered that was just the beginning. I served God doing the 'right things' and in 1998 God called me to attend a Pentecostal Bible College. During my three years at college I learnt a wealth of great information and theory but I wasn't taught about my identity in God. I gained a theological degree and great foundation for ministry. I acquired good biblical doctrine but it did not transform my heart nor did it provide the platform for gaining the revelation of what it is to be a child of God.[1] After my three years I graduated, got married, relocated, and my wife and I jumped head first into helping to lead a small church plant.

All I did to serve Him was from a place of wanting to gain approval; I was not serving from a place of sonship. Sonship is a revelation of the heart which brings us to a place of relationship with the Father, living in the family of God. It was not from a place of knowing who I was, that I was a child of God. It was as if I was doing it because that was what was expected of me. I was helping from a place of orphan thinking.[2] I was busy. I was happy to do whatever was asked of me. I thought I was doing the right things. But once I began my journey of understanding who I am in Him I realised that my service, although good, was not from a place of rest. By nature I am someone who 'does'. If there is something to be done, I am willing to do it, but I began to realise that my motives were wrong. Father lovingly and gently showed me that when I had done whatever it was I was doing I would seek the approval and acceptance of the person I had been serving. I thought if I just do this thing or complete that task, then I would be liked more, I would feel as though I had earned something. Father showed me that He loves me no matter what I do or don't do. His love for me is complete now. There is nothing I can do that will cause Him to love me more. Similarly the reverse is true; there is nothing I can do to make Him love me less. I have learnt that His love for me is not dependent on anything I do.

---

[1] I am always grateful for my time at Bible College; I met some amazing people and made lifelong friends. I would also encourage anyone who is thinking of going into any kind of biblical ministry to attend some biblical training.

[2] In the chapter Co-heirs with Christ, I will look more into what it is to have orphan thinking and what it is to be in sonship.

His love for me is only reliant upon His unchanging nature. It is impossible for Him to act in any way that is contrary to His nature.

I vividly remember a time when Father was taking me through a really tough season. I felt disengaged. I felt really alone. I felt as though the approval I was wanting from others, I was not receiving. I felt let down by everyone. Looking back I can see this was really the embryonic stages of Him dealing with my heart. It was over time as Father continued to show me love and grace that my heart slowly began the healing process as He showed me the attitude of my heart. He began to reveal to me that I was seeking others' approval, that I was looking for love from people rather than the love that only He can bring, I was able to identify that I had an orphan heart. He showed me that all I was looking for was from orphan thinking. With His continued love and total acceptance of me, I was then able to move from this place of having an orphan mindset to one of sonship.

I recall one evening when I was leading a small group where I said 'I know God loves me.' However, after being on this journey I now realise I had not fully understood the depth of what that really meant, it was at this stage in my life only head knowledge.

My journey into sonship began whilst driving home from work listening to the song 'No Longer Slaves' by Jonathan and Melissa Helser. One line began to capture my heart, "I am a child of God". As I listened to this line over and over, it was like Father was searing my heart with this truth and my heart was being branded with that one phrase. I began to allow the truth of what I was hearing and singing to not just envelop my heart but my entire being. It was like I was being changed from the inside out. I can now say with full conviction that God loves me and that I am a child of God.

It was only as I allowed the Father to take me on this journey of understanding what it means to be in the image of God that He began to melt my heart and allow the head knowledge of His love to trickle down to my heart and allow me to fully experience the immense love He has for me. I began to feel more of His compassion for me, more of the deep affection He has for me and as this took place, my heart became lighter. Some of the burdens and hurts from the past began to literally melt away. He began to heal me and as this happened I was filled with His love for me, and a new joy and a new peace entered my life. Part of this process took place as I received prayer ministry, called Bethel Sozo[3]. It was during one of these sessions that Father showed me my orphan heart. He showed me that I was operating from a place of seeking approval, He showed me that I had become independent of Him. He revealed this was not His best for me; He wanted me to be dependent on Him. He revealed to me where this had first started in my life, and through a process of forgiving others and the revealing of truths He was showing me about who He is, that I was able to allow Him an all access pass to my heart. I was able to let Him gently and lovingly bring me from having an orphan mindset to one of sonship.

When the Father began to reveal to me that I had an orphan heart, I had previously thought an orphan was a person without any surviving parents. It was only when the Father took the

---

[3] Sozo is an inner healing ministry tool developed by Bethel Church, Redding, California. The word Sozo is the Greek word that is used in the New Testament which means: Saved, Healed and Delivered.

time to show me what it meant for a believer to have an orphan mindset did I realise that it was possible for me as a believer to have an orphan heart. I had not previously thought of Christians as having a spiritual orphan heart. It was a concept I had never come across before. As I learnt more about Christians living with this heart condition I began to realise that children, due to not having parents, may have become independent. Some of the consequences linked to this are feelings of having to do things on your own. With the orphan heart and the consequences attached to it we feel as though we have no-one there for us and so we may put up barriers because we think that life is about protecting ourselves and what we can get from life. Life becomes all about 'me' and we begin to resent others telling us what to do or suggesting other ways of doing something. Those with this thinking often do not accept they have a home and any sense of belonging is something that does not fit well with them. Often orphans feel as though they don't have a place of belonging, a place they can feel safe.

I began to realise that my relationships were affected by this way of thinking. I began to question if my relationships were real or were they more for my selfish gain? Were my relationships genuine and for the mutual benefit of others and myself or were they more for my own personal need? Whilst I do believe the majority of my relationships were not primarily based on what I could receive, there were times when out of my orphan thinking, I used my friendships to get something from them in order to feel better about myself. The effects of having an orphan heart have implications on how we treat others and how we allow others to treat us. Our hearts can become hard and our lives become independent of others.

During my journeying with Father about my orphan heart to transitioning into my identity being in Him, He showed me that I had compared myself to others and that this is unhelpful because I am who I am; I am made in the image of God. Therefore I have a purpose and because I am made in His image, then I am who He wants me to be. He is not looking for me to be somebody else. He is looking for me to be the best me I can be; the me He created me to be.

Father showed me a lot of my thinking was from my orphan heart. I had never stopped to consider my lifelong way of thinking. I had never really considered I might have wrong thought patterns, or that I believed lies from the enemy. When we believe these lies, we are actually partnering with them. It is like we are saying we are in agreement with them and consequently we empower them and give them permission to affect us.

As I grow further into sonship I can now look back and see that my previous way of thinking was all about me and about what I could get from other people. Acceptance and love were the main things I was trying to get and not what I might be able to give to them. The motivations in my relationships were selfish. They were about me.

I attended a Father Heart conference in March 2015 and Father began to speak to me in a vision. I saw an angel and it was as if he was pointing to me. I soon realised that the angel was not actually looking at me; rather he was asking Father if I was the one. Father said: "Yes, he is the one, I am well pleased with him, I love him, he is My child." At this point I was unable to stand, all I could do was lay down under the heaviness of His presence. I received revelation and realised that Father was so pleased with me He was telling the angelic host about me, who I was, that He was excited by me and I realised that I was accepted by my Father in Heaven. I began to realise that I did have a home, a home with Him. I understood that He was my Father.

Through another vision the Father began to speak to me. He said how pleased He is with me and that He was melting my heart for Him, giving me a greater capacity to receive His love and a greater understanding of who I am in Him. He said that I carry His glory and His presence. He said His study is always open to me. He always wants me to visit Him. He has time for me. This was new for me, Father God, who created the Heavens and the earth, not only loves me, but wants to spend time with me, He always has time for me, he is never too busy for me. He continued by saying that He would cause me to be able to carry more of His presence, He said to me "you are not able to stand too much right now but I want you to carry a greater portion of My presence". I realised I do that by spending more time with Father God, allowing His thoughts of who I am to become my thoughts, to ensure my beliefs about me agree with His beliefs and therefore are truth about me.

I was at another conference about 8 months later, when Father again began to speak to me. He showed me more of His love for me; Father gave me another vision where He showed me very powerfully the amazing love He has for me. It started simply where He took me for a walk along a beach and we played in the sea having fun. Then suddenly the scene changed to a garden, we continued walking in the garden where Father stopped and picked a beautiful flower and gave it to me. I was struck by the type and colour of the flower; it was a white rose. As I began to ponder the importance of a white rose it was like the rest of the vision had been leading to this one significant action. I asked Father why a white rose? Again He just showed me it. The vision ended but I was so captivated by this rose that I did a little research into white roses. I discovered that the white rose was traditionally known as the bridal rose, it was the original wedding flower, it was the early symbol of true love. I also discovered it is a symbol of not just purity, but also innocence, sympathy, and spirituality. It was during this time that Father showed me, not just in my head, but my heart too, that I was His bride and that His love for me was perfect and true. He showed me just how pure and spotless His love for me really is, not only am I His bride, but I too am innocent because His love for me has literally washed me clean. The vision and the meaning of the flower impacted me for the next couple of days and every time I thought about it I would become a crying wreck. The vision of the white rose and its meaning profoundly affected who I was. It transformed my way of thinking. However, during a time of doubt, where the enemy tried to come and steal all Father had shown me, I said to Father, if that was really you, allow someone else to have a similar picture for me. That same evening my wife and I were praying with some friends and their 8 year old daughter came to pray for me. The girl said she had a picture of me falling into some flowers, when I asked her what type of flowers they were she said that they were roses; I didn't need to ask the colour. Father was so keen for me to grasp this revelation; He is so loving and kind that He used a young girl to confirm how He really thinks of me. If ever I begin to question the love of the Father and what I mean to Him, He simply reminds me of this beautiful picture.

Again I was at small conference, when I had a vision of me worshipping with the angels. Suddenly Jesus appeared in all of His glory. I became aware that the angels were beginning to bow their knees, within the vision I sensed that I needed to do the same. The glorious majestic King of Kings had entered the room and the only thing to do was bow. As I went to bow, Jesus said "No, you don't need to bow." He took me for a walk. As we were walking we approached a large fountain, Jesus said either go through the fountain or around it. I decided to go through it and as I went through the fountain I felt an overwhelming peace, a peace that to this day I simply cannot describe. It was peace mixed with complete love. As I have continued on this journey of understanding His great love for me and what that actually means I have continued to grow in my revelation of what it means to be in His Image, to be a child of God, to be an heir, and co-heir with Christ; I can honestly say that I am not the same. My thinking has changed, my attitude has changed, I am secure in who I am as a person, I am at a place of rest. I am not someone who generally thinks from a place of orphan thinking anymore as I have been transformed by His love, my thinking is now from my identity as a child of God, being His son.

As I have grown in my understanding of who I am, I have also grown in intimacy with Father. I have always been someone who loves to worship God. I sense and enjoy His presence in worship. I have begun to understand more about the importance of worship, not least because of something that Father spoke to me about whilst I was worshipping. He spoke to me saying "Heaven is awoken by our worship, our worship causes hell to tremble." He said, "when the lion roars all hell trembles. Actually when you roar, you make hell tremble and shake." I was confused by this. I understood that angels worship Him, so what was so special about our worship? I asked Father about this, His response though simple, blew me away. He said "Angels are made to worship, you choose to worship, and that is the difference. That is why Heaven is awoken by your worship." I saw the power of our worship. I understood we have a choice; we can either choose to not worship, or we can choose to worship. I began to understand that as we are loved by the Father, when we as His children choose to return that love back to Him through the simple act of worship, there is a power that hell cannot stand. Any good earthly father loves to hear their children say "I love you daddy" and as such the father responds. It is only as we choose to turn the love back onto Him, and declare our love for Him through worship, that causes all of Heaven to take note, it causes something in the Heavens to respond. It is like the roar of a lion. It is a battle cry that causes the enemy to fear. He is hearing God's children declaring that they are loved by the Father. Satan is hearing the sound of defeat. I began to understand that our worship opens something of Heaven and releases it on earth. I believe as we continue to worship Him and He is attracted to our worship that this then releases something of the Kingdom and it must by default usher in His presence.

Father spoke to me about the power of His presence and about hosting His presence. It started by Father saying: "When you live in My presence you live a life of power". Before this journey began of understanding who I am in Him, I often used the following phrase 'practice His presence'. I had described the idea of practising His presence as something we can learn and whilst we can and should learn to host His presence,

Father asked me "How can you practice my presence? To see if we get on? When you want to spend time with friends don't you just invite them round and they come? It's just natural, you sit, and you chat". He showed me that when we have our friends round and we host them we don't practice first, we just have them round. Father was saying it is not possible to 'practice His presence'. Either His presence is with us or it is not. Ultimately He wants us to spend more time acknowledging His presence and living in an awareness of the reality of His presence.

How often do we have the perception that if we just do this or do that, then maybe God will show up? I believe this is a religious spirit. The Bible says, "Draw near to God and He will draw near to you" (James 4:8a). All we have to do is make time for His presence. He promises to then draw near to us. There is nothing that suggests we have to follow any principle or guidelines for Him to fulfil His promise.

Father showed me that the idea of thinking we are not good enough; the thought we have to pray more, read the Bible more, or have more quiet times to somehow make us better Christians is a lie from the devil. Whilst these are all good disciplines, actually all Father is looking for are our open hearts; hearts that are open to His presence and to seeing and allowing Him to do what He wants in our lives in His timing.

With all that I have said, however, there are times when His presence appears to be more manifest than others. Have you ever walked into a room, such as I once did and realised that something was taking place; that God was present and moving? For me it felt as though if I had spoken it would have broken the presence. It would have broken the peace. These are times

I believe Father wants to increase in us; He too wants to manifest His presence amongst us more. He is just looking for wiling hearts that say "Come, Lord Jesus, come! More Lord!"

I believe the more we acknowledge His presence, the more we spend time with Him, the more we will see of His manifest presence. Father began to show me when we spend time with Him things have to change. This was after I had been suffering with a heavy cold and it just disappeared as I decided to spend time in His presence. When something of His eternal Kingdom invades, or even just touches something of our earthly realm, there is a shift that takes place and the eternal pushes out the earthly.

Maybe you have heard of what takes place in His presence and thought "I want more of that". Maybe you have seen the effect of Him in people's lives and thought "I want what they have". Maybe you have even dipped your toe in to try and experience this for yourself, but as you dip in, something comes against you, something knocks you a bit and it causes you to be frightened or not so sure. The initial excitement fades as the fear or uncertainty kicks in.

I would encourage you to continue to press in and enjoy His company. I encourage you to seek Him and spend time with Him and just allow Him to reveal and do what He wants. Why not just come to Him with no agenda, with no prayer requests and just be with Him? I have on many occasions done just that. I have some worship music on in the background, I have just sat, maybe sung along to the worship, but my focus has been on opening myself up to Him and as promised, He always comes. Often, I just sit and listen to what He wants to say to me. As I listen He whispers His feelings towards me and the thoughts He has for me. I listen to what He wants to teach me and what He wants to show me. These times are so special. They are a time of intimacy as He reveals His heart for me. Of course there is a risk that this in itself could become a formula, but the moment it does, our open and willing hearts will not be so open and willing.

You might say "but you don't know what is going on in my life…". I agree I don't, but I am sure that Father knows all of the details of your life intimately and He will continue to say "The Lord will fight for you; you only need to be still" (Exodus 14:14). The Psalmist encourages us to "Be still before the Lord and wait patiently for Him" (Psalms 37:7) or as the song writer puts is "Be still for the presence of the Lord is all around"

Father also began to speak to me about what it means to "be still". He began to show me that to be still in the Lord is to rest in Him. He showed me that resting in Him is like when He rested from His work in Genesis 2. The idea of resting here is not about being tired, but the word is more about being satisfied with the work that He had accomplished. He said to be still, or to rest in Him, is more about being satisfied in His presence. When we rest in His presence, we are satisfied there is nothing better to do. When we are still with Him, we are allowing Him to work through our situations. They are being dealt with by Him rather than by us. What does it mean to be satisfied in His presence? It means to be happy and conclude that nothing more can be done, that there is nowhere better to be.

When my wife and I were preparing to move to Malawi things were going well when all of a sudden the door to moving to Malawi that had appeared to have opened up for us out of nowhere was firmly slammed in our faces. Our route into the country was no more and it looked as though our plans would have to be put on hold. I remember during this time of uncertainty that Father really gave me peace as I rested in Him. Somehow I knew it was going to be ok. Father was saying to me "I've got this. You are my son, I love you, and I will fight your battles for you." What the enemy wanted was to steal my peace. He wanted me to question our move to Malawi. He wanted me to doubt our ministry in Malawi, but Father once again showed Himself to be faithful. He showed Himself to be a true loving Father. He proved to me that just as He had called us, so He was with us all the way.

I have learnt that as we progress through the journey of discovering who we are, that we are totally and unconditionally loved by the Father. This does not distract the enemy, it does not stop him from battling with us, but the more we understand the Father's unconditional love for us we are better able to see the enemy for who he is and we can fight from the place of abiding in Father's love, we can do this knowing that the Father is for us.

The journey I have been on is a continuous one. I have discovered there is always more of His love that can be revealed to us. There is more we can always learn about who we are. I am not sure I ever thought once my wife and I moved to Malawi we would be all sorted, that we had nothing else to learn, but even if the idea even entered my head, I would have been totally wrong! I learn daily the new things He wants to bring to me, increasing my capacity to understand in richer detail, with new insights of all the things it means to be in His image. One such occasion was whilst we were waiting to receive our visas to be able to live longer term in the country.

We had been waiting for about a year for the Immigration Department in Malawi to approve our application and whilst I was listening to Bethel's song "God of Miracles" Father spoke to me very clearly. He said that when things go well you don't require faith. It is a journey to learn to trust Him; it is a journey to grow in faith. He asked me, "Do you trust me?" Instinctively I responded "Yes". Then Father caused me to think about Bethel and I began to think it is easy for them, when they see miracles all the time. It is easy for them to sing "He's a God of miracles, I believe in you."

Father showed me very clearly that whilst my head said yes I trust you, my heart was not quite there yet. He said to me it was not always like that for Bethel. He showed me that singing a declaration song like that shows where things are. He showed me that despite the circumstances we can sing a song of declaration, because we know God is bigger than our circumstances, God does not change. He is the God of miracles. He asked me if I was willing to sing or even able to sing the song and believe it even when miracles don't happen.

It is a journey that will last; Father showed me it is a place of hope. He showed me I am desperate to see the miracles that we are to experience, therefore being in a place of seeking, a place of asking, a place of questioning is good. If I were not doing these things, If I were not questioning, if I were not asking and seeking then I would not be bothered about miracles. He challenged me; He is a God of miracles. I believe in Him, He is the God of miracles. I know that. It is true.

He said it is a process, it is a journey of learning and of growing for me, to be able to declare the truth, even when miracles don't appear to happen. He said Bethel started somewhere, we all start somewhere, but the point is that we are moving forward. The more we declare the truth the more our spirits will line up with the Heavenly truth. The more our spirits line up with the Heavenly truth, the more we will see miracles. In fact these times of testing are a time for us to cling to Him, so we can look back and believe Him for even greater miracles as we continue to believe for more.

Father does not want us to be pulled down by our circumstances, He does not want us to be distracted by our situation, He wants us to be in that place where we believe He is a God of miracles, and He is the one who does the impossible. He wants us to look to Him. He wants us to believe in Him.

No matter what we are going through we should declare it over our lives, we should declare it over our situation. Our circumstances do not dictate to God, but He dictates to our circumstances. He is bigger than anything we face. It is His grace that is sufficient (2 Corinthians 12:9). Believe it. Hold on to it. Trust it. Declare it.

No matter where on our journey we are, He is the same. He is the one who can. Believe for what you can now. Trust Him. It might be too big for you, but it is not too big for the God of miracles. Start to declare over your life that you are a child of God. Declare that you are loved by Him. When we declare something we are making a statement that this is true. As we begin to make these declarations over our lives we are stating that what we are saying is true. It might be that you don't believe it, that you don't fully understand it, but do it anyway and watch how your spirit begins to align with the truth of what Father thinks about you. My journey began by using this

Mark Russell

simple process of repeatedly declaring one line "I am a child of God" and I now know it to be true.

In His Image

Identity

Before we begin to look at what it means to be in His image, it is necessary to understand why our identity is such an important issue. Unless we know who we are, we will never grasp how essential it is to be in His image. Being in His image I believe is the most important thing there is in relation to understanding our true identity. When we know this we can then begin to understand where our true identity comes from. We need to know where our identity currently lies and what the influences on our identity are. This could be our friends or work colleagues, our family, maybe even our church leaders. However, I believe that if this is the case then we are looking to the wrong source from where we draw our identity from. There are many reasons why we might be looking to the wrong place, but it is time to move our focus and adjust our thinking to ensure we are getting our identity from the one source in whom we should be getting our true identity from, Father God. We need to see ourselves as He sees us; we need to be rooted in the truth of His thoughts about us. We need to know what He thinks and feels about us. Once this happens we can begin to experience the love that He has for us and so our love for Him will grow deeper too.

Since the very beginning satan has been trying to take the place of God. Satan saw himself as beautiful, intelligent and with great power and position (Ezekiel 28:17). This caused him to desire for himself the honour and glory which is due to God. This was his rebellion against God and as a result this was the very thing that got him thrown out of Heaven.

"I saw satan fall like lightning from Heaven…"

Luke 10:18

It is interesting to note the very thing we have is the very thing satan wants; to be made in God's image (Genesis 1:27). He is tormented by us every day because he sees in us what he has always wanted to become. As a result it is the tactic of satan to cause us to question our identity. He has been attacking who we really are since the days of Adam and Eve. Whether you have heard this teaching before or if this teaching is relatively new to you, it is not new to him; it is however one of the main weapons that he uses against us as he attacks our identity. He does all he can to keep our true identity hidden from us.

Let's look at where it went wrong in the Garden of Eden.

The very first temptation by satan recorded in the Bible was to question what God had said about not eating the forbidden fruit:

"Did God really say, 'you shall not eat from any tree in the garden?'"

Genesis 3:1b

It was the purpose of the devil to cause Eve, and therefore mankind, to question what God had said. Once mankind began to question, it was a simple process to cause us to doubt God's integrity and subsequently for us to doubt our identity. The thought process goes something like this: God is withholding something from you, therefore He cannot be trusted. This in turn leads us to question our own identity, and what it really means to be made in His image.[1] The truth is God cannot lie (Hebrews 6:18) and if He says we are made in His image then we are made in His image.

"So God created man in His own image, in the image of God He created Him; male and female He created them."

Genesis 1:27

The original deception from the enemy, which was a subtle one, it is one whereby mankind is caused to question our identity.

Once we begin to question our identity, which can happen over a period of time, just as the lie to Eve was subtle so the lie which we believe can also be subtle. Once this happens we begin to believe the labels of our false identities. These labels are the words people say about us.

The labels we carry are projected on to us by people we know; maybe our parents, friends, work colleagues or maybe our church pastor. Examples of labels can include: we are worthless, we will never amount to anything, maybe someone has said you are stupid or ugly. Over time you may have felt

---

[1] Puttman, R. (2013) *School of Kingdom Ministry Manual.* Coaching Saints Publications. p.84. (Permission granted)

shame because of what this person or people may have said to you, you feel like a failure. The list could go on and on.

Whatever the label is and whoever said those things to you, ultimately any negative labels are lies that have been given to us by satan, as a way for us to think of ourselves differently to what God thinks about us. These labels bind us up and determine how we see ourselves. For example, if you carry the label that you are failure then when you are asked to do something you may not try your very best, you think to yourself there is no point. After all you know you are going to fail anyway. Or you might suggest that someone else be identified to do that task as you are not good at whatever it might be. The negative labels we carry ultimately limit our ability and our destiny and stop us flourishing in all that God has for us. Just as a plant needs water, sunlight and oxygen to do well, if any of these are removed its growth is hindered and it stops flourishing. It is similar to us, we need to see ourselves as God sees us or else we too will find ourselves not thriving.

These labels form part of our identity. They become who we are as over time we begin to partner with these labels and enter into agreement with them.

We began this chapter by looking at the temptation of Eve and how she was tricked into questioning her true identity. I propose that the devil has continued, since creation, to cause us to question who we are. Let us look at the life of Jesus, in particular His baptism:

"When all the people were being baptised, Jesus was baptised too. And as He was praying, Heaven opened and the Holy Spirit descended on Him in

*bodily form like a dove. And a voice came from Heaven: "You are **my Son**, whom **I love**; with you I am **well pleased**."*

Luke 3:21-22 (emphasis added)

We can see clearly here that Jesus was baptised, not just with water and the Holy Spirit, but He also received a baptism of love from His Father. He received from the Father an understanding of who He was. He received His identity. His identity is made of three things; He is God's Son, He is loved by the Father, and finally the Father is pleased with Him.

It is worth noting that immediately after Jesus' baptism His identity is challenged, He is faced with the question of who He really is.

*"Jesus, full of the Holy Spirit, returned from the Jordan and was led by the Spirit into the desert, where for forty days He was tempted by the devil. He ate nothing during those days, and at the end of them He was hungry. The devil said to Him, **"If you are the Son of God**, tell this stone to become bread." Jesus answered, "It is written: 'Man shall not live on bread alone.'" The devil led Him up to a high place and showed Him in an instant all the kingdoms of the world. And he said to Him, "I will give you all their authority and splendour; it has been given to me, and I can give it to anyone I want to. If you worship me, it will all be yours." Jesus answered, "It is written: 'Worship the Lord your God and serve Him only.'" The devil led Him to Jerusalem and had Him stand on the highest point of the temple. **"If you are the Son of God**," he said, "throw yourself down from here. For it is written: "'He will command His angels concerning you to guard you carefully; they will lift you up in their hands, so that you will not strike your foot against a stone.'" Jesus answered, "It is said: 'Do not put the Lord your God to the test.'" When the devil had finished all this tempting, he left Him until an opportune time."*

Luke 4:1-13 (emphasis added)

Notice that satan uses the same trick as he did with Eve, he says "if you are the Son of God". He is attempting to cause Jesus to doubt what His Father said, in the same way he caused Eve to doubt way back in Genesis 3:1. Jesus was firm in who He was, He knew exactly who His Father was and how His Father felt about Him. Jesus was fully aware of who He was to His Father and how much He meant to Him. He was able to rest in the knowledge of the truth about what His Father thought about Him and who He was. It is interesting to note that at this point Jesus had not completed any work, He had not taken part in any ministry. No healings had taken place, no miracles had been performed. Jesus was not having to face the question of whether He had done something well enough or if He could have preached that sermon better; His work ethic was not being questioned. First and foremost for Jesus was to know who He was and what His Father thought and felt about Him.

When we have a false understanding of who we are I believe several things can happen which we will look at next. The reverse is also true, that when we fully know our identity in Christ then a release begins to happen and we begin to find ourselves becoming free of those labels. Therefore let us look at some of the things that happen when we have a wrong perception of our identity.

Bondage

A wrong identity holds us in bondage; we are tied up in a lie. Have you ever tried to untie a really tight knot? If you don't pull at the correct part of that knot then often the knot becomes tighter, often it is the same with the lies we believe.

The more we try to break ourselves free, the tighter the hold becomes and so it appears there is nothing we can do, which in turn might cause us to eventually give up. Our own attempts will fail.

However, when we understand our true identity in Him something amazing happens, it brings us into freedom. The Bible is very clear that the truth shall set us free (John 8:32). When we know the truth of who we are we begin to be liberated and are no longer in bondage to that lie anymore. We are able to stand up and come out of agreement with the lie and accept the truth. Where once the lie held us it no longer has the power to do so, and so it loses its grip and we are able to break free.

Prisoner

When we have a wrong understanding of our identity we become prisoners, it may feel like we can only see the bars or the lies around us. Very often we don't even realise we are believing a lie until it is fully explained to us. A prison is for those who are found guilty of whatever they have been accused of. As we become imprisoned in the lie we are believing, we take on that false identity and become convinced we are guilty and therefore live as though we are.

However it is also true to say that some people are falsely imprisoned. The truth is we are falsely imprisoned by the label, the false identity is not ours to wear. We have been falsely accused because when we have a true identity we become fully released, the prison doors are no longer locked shut, they are opened. We can walk out; we are fully released free children of God. The truth becomes like a key, and we can use the truth of who we are to unlock the prison door, we are able to walk out as free children.

"So if the Son sets you free, you will be free indeed"

John 8:36

Striving

When we believe a false identity about ourselves it can cause us to strive or work harder and better, we do all we can in our own effort to prove ourselves. Sadly, the truth is the more we try to do things by our own effort and the more we try to prove to ourselves and others, the more we become embedded in the lie. It feels like there is nothing we can do, we never feel like what we are doing is working, we never become satisfied. It appears that we are in a vicious circle of striving, never meeting our own or others' expectations. It is worth reminding ourselves again that Jesus received His identity from His Father before He had done anything.

Living out our true identity enables us to rest as we no longer have to prove anything to anyone. We don't have to try to be better or work harder to make a point. We are fully aware that no matter what happens our Father in Heaven loves us. As we saw a moment ago, at the point that Jesus received His identity He had done nothing, He had not completed any miracle nor had He raised anyone from the dead. He received His identity at the beginning of His ministry and not at the end when He had done all that was required of Him. Everything Jesus did was out of knowing who He was. Jesus did everything He did from a place of rest and from a place of a true understanding of His identity. Knowing who He was enabled Him to work from a place of rest with the Father rather than working for the

Father. When we know who we are we stop working to please other people, we stop working for them and we know that Father is pleased with us no matter what.

Hopelessness

An incorrect identity can make us feel hopeless; it makes us feel there is no point in anything, we become disheartened and discouraged and so we give up. We may say something like "what is the point?", or "why am I bothering?" and so the false identity begins to grip us all the more and we look at everything with a negative attitude. We begin to think 'Why me?' and we start to compare ourselves to others and we see all the negative things in our lives.

However with a true identity things are very different. We have hope; we don't question but we feel better about things we do. We look at things with a much more positive attitude, instead of the glass half empty attitude, we have a mentality of the glass half full. We see things as though they can get better, it might not be great now, but that is not going to stop me. We are focused once again on Him, the one true source for our lives. Where once we felt hopeless, hope is restored and we can hold our head high and our faith begins to rise.

Insecurity

A false identity makes us feel insecure, it causes us to question what we do and why we do things. So we might seek the approval of others and we ask others what they thought. Sadly, no matter what people say it is never enough and so we look back on what we have done and think of ways we could have done it better. We don't look at the good, we only focus on the negative. We question ourselves and we question others, but there is never anything that makes us feel secure. We might even try and bring others to the same level we are at and discourage them. When we are insecure we may find ourselves looking down, we might find it hard to make eye contact with people because we are ashamed of who we are.

The good news is the true identity provides us with security because not only do we know who we are, we also know whose we are. It allows us to question in a good way, we see the positive a lot more than the negative. We no longer seek the approval of others; we understand that the approval of others will not change anything. We understand that our identity comes from the Father and He alone is the one we get our approval from. With a correct understanding of this we know that Father is always pleased with us, He is always looking upon us with pride. Instead of bringing others down we want to build others up. We want to encourage others and see the good in others. We are able to walk around with our head held high.

Wrong Focus

We should understand that the false identities we carry ultimately come from one place, they come from the enemy. He is the one who does not want you to know who you really are. Therefore as a result our focus is on those things that he says, and an incorrect understanding of who we are might cause us to focus on the person where we first got that identity from. When we have a false identity, and therefore a wrong focus, we tend to look at who we think we are rather than look at who God says we are. I once heard Bill Johnson say in a talk: "I cannot afford to have a thought in my head about me that God doesn't have in His."

However, a true identity makes us focus on the Father. The One who we get our identity from is the One we want to please; therefore He becomes our focus.

When we have a correct understanding of who we are we are dangerous to the enemy because we know that the lies he tries to feed us do not line up with what our Heavenly Father thinks about us. Therefore our behaviour and how we act flows out from that identity.

Just as when a prisoner is freed from prison, the first thing he does is take off the prison clothes, the clothes that say he was a prisoner, he becomes a new man, he has become free. Paul says that we put on our new self by making new the attitude of our minds (Ephesians 4:23-24). Also in Romans Paul puts it like this:

> *"Do not conform any longer to the pattern of this world, but be **transformed by the renewing of your mind**."*
>
> *Romans 12:2 (emphasis added)*

Renewing our mind is changing the way we think to the way God thinks. It includes changing the way we think about ourselves to the way God thinks about us and who we are. It is like our minds and our way of thinking are put back to the original blueprint of how we were made. The prisoner when he is free has to change the way his thinks, he now has to think as a free man, not as someone who is bound by the rules of the prison.

Bill Johnson puts it like this:

It is not just our thoughts that are different, but that our way of thinking is transformed because we think from a different reality – from Heaven towards earth! That is the transformed perspective.[2]

It is time to let go of our old identities and those labels that people have placed on us that have held us back and renew our minds. It is time to believe the truth about what the Father thinks of us, it is time to see ourselves from the perspective of Heaven. It is time to see ourselves as God sees us, as He originally made us.

Let's take a look at blind Bartimaeus:

> "Then they came to Jericho. As Jesus and His disciples, together with a large crowd, were leaving the city, **a blind man**, Bartimaeus (that is, the Son of Timaeus), was sitting by the roadside begging. When he heard that it was Jesus of Nazareth, he began to shout, "Jesus, Son of David, have mercy on me!" Many rebuked him and told him to be quiet, but he shouted all the more, "Son of David, have mercy on me!" Jesus stopped and said, "Call him." **So they called to the blind man**, "Cheer up! On your feet! He's calling you." **Throwing his cloak aside**, he jumped to his feet and came to Jesus. "What do you want me to do for you?" Jesus asked him. **The blind man** said, "Rabbi, I want to see." "Go," said Jesus, "Your faith has healed you." Immediately he received his sight and **followed Jesus along the road**."
>
> Mark 10:46-52 (emphasis added)

Bartimaeus literally had the label 'blind'; notice in verse 46 his label comes first and was therefore how he was known. His

---

[2] Johnson, B. (2005) *The Supernatural Power of a Transformed Mind.* Shippensburg: Destiny Image. p.42. (Permission Granted)

label became his identity. Three times he is called blind (verse 46, verse 49 and verse 51), but only once is his name used. It is interesting to note that Jesus never called Bartimaeus blind, Jesus never called Bartimaeus by his label. Jesus never agrees with the wrong labels we carry, the false identities we have of ourselves and He will never call us by those false names. He calls us by who we are and not who we have become. He knows our true identities; He calls us by those only.

I would like us to note another thing about this passage. In verse 50, we read "Throwing his cloak aside". This was not just an ordinary cloak. In this time people had the right to beg if they had the agreement from the government; if you like his wearing the coat legitimised who he was. Not only did Bartimaeus literally have the label, but in effect he literally carried the label with him wherever he went. However, Bartimaeus threw his cloak aside before he came to Jesus, before he was able to see he recognised something in who Jesus was, he understood that coming to Jesus would mean a new identity. There was a faith that said Jesus can give me a new identity, in this case he would no longer be blind. He now had a new identity, he could no longer be called blind, he left his cloak and followed Jesus in verse 52 Bartimaeus was now walking in his new identity, he did not go back to get his cloak.

The false identities we carry are lies, they are not the truth of who we are. They come from satan, who is described by Jesus in John's gospel as "a liar and the father of lies" (John 8:44). We renew our minds by rejecting the lies we have believed, recognising them for what they are, and by starting to agree with the truth. In the book of Hebrews we read "it is impossible for God to lie." (Hebrew 6:18).

So what are the truths of who the Father says we are? What is our true identity? There are many and this book deals with just some of them. For the purposes of this chapter I want to look at the identity that the Father gave to Jesus, and therefore has given to us as His children:

You are my son

> *"You are my Son, whom I love; with you I am well pleased."*
>
> *Luke 3:22*

Firstly the Father says "you are my Son". This was the first identity of who Jesus is, He is the Son of God. As we read the New Testament we discover that we too are sons [3]. We are His children. We will look more in depth at this later.

> *"For you did not receive a spirit that makes you a slave again to fear, but you received the Spirit of sonship. And by Him we cry, "Abba, Father.""*
>
> *Romans 8:15*

Whom I love

The second identity the Father says about Jesus is "whom I love". Not only did the Father say Jesus was His Son but also that He loved Him. This is true of us too, this is our identity.

> *"How great is the love the Father has lavished on us, that we should be called children of God! And that is what we are"*
>
> *1 John 3:1*

---

[3] In biblical thinking the word 'sons' does not always denote gender. It is more understood to be one who depends on another.

The Father has so much love for us that He lavishes it on us, He pours it all over us; there is no end to the devotion He has for us. There is nothing we can do to stop that deep affection and there is nothing we can do to make Him love us more. Whether we feel like He loves us or whether we don't, the fact remains, we are loved by Him. As John says "that is who we are". We are loved children of God. TRUTH!

I make the assumption that we all know God loves us, but I have discovered that knowing as a fact or piece of information in our minds is different to knowing in our hearts. A friend of mine refers to knowing in our hearts as "knowing in our knower." In other words, we just know. We know because we know, because we know. It is no longer head knowledge; it is something we can experience. It is a truth that is so deep and so real that it just cannot be removed from us.

With you I am well pleased

Thirdly we read that the Father is pleased. "…with you I am well pleased". Again it is worth reminding ourselves that at this point Jesus had not completed any miracles nor had he completed any ministry. Jesus at this point had kept a low profile, but still the Father says He is pleased with Him. So often people have a false belief that if they complete this task, or work in this way, then He will be pleased with us. Just as Jesus had done nothing, so too is it true of us.

Just like expectant parents who have wanted to start a family, they love their child as soon they know they have conceived. This child has not done anything, the child is simply loved. The love the parents feel after the birth is so strong it can almost hurt.

Let us read these two passages:

*"His pleasure is not in the strength of the horse, not His delight in the legs of a man; the Lord **delights** in those who fear Him, who put their hope in His unfailing love."*

Psalm 147:10-11 (emphasis added)

Also:

*"And without faith it is impossible to **please** God, because anyone who comes to Him must believe that He exists and that He rewards those who earnestly seek Him."*

Hebrews 11:6 (emphasis added)

Notice in these two passages it appears that all we have to do for the Father to be pleased with us is believe that He exists, in other words, have faith. He is delighted with us or pleased with us when we simply believe in Him. In the passage from Psalms, the idea of fearing is not one of trembling, but rather it should be understood as one who worships Him. In other words one who puts his faith in Him.

In both passages there is no mention of any works to be completed or certain tasks accomplished; it is not about how many people we have won for Jesus, it is not about how many people we have prayed for on the street. There is also no mention of any other conditions required. It is simply a matter of saying "I put my hope in you." Or more simply the moment we give our life to Him, the moment we follow Him, then He is pleased with us.

We have been given all we need. Our identity is found only in Him. All we have to do is take hold of it, after all it has been given freely. Therefore we do not have to work for it, we can stop striving. As sons of the Father there is no longer a need to find our identity in doing, but it is simply found in being a son of the Father.

To fully understand and appreciate our identity is a revelatory process. Our minds and hearts need to be renewed to grasp the full truth. Knowledge is only part of the story, we need to have a revelation of the truth of that knowledge. Knowledge affects the head whereas revelation affects the heart, and the heart is where any true change can take place. The following quote from R Puttman explains the concept that it is only by revelation that the heart can change.

> *"Revelation releases an impartation and leads to transformation. Knowledge releases information and leads to education. Revelation releases in the heart the capacity to live out what the mind is seeing."* [4]

Having read this far you may be thinking how do we stop believing the lying tongue of the enemy? How do we start to renew our minds in such a way that we start to believe the things the Father says about us?

I believe there are four simple things we can do:[5]

Repent

Firstly we should repent and turn away from the lies we have listened to and agreed with. Repentance in the Bible means to turn, the idea being that we turn away from. Another meaning

---

[4] Puttman, R. (2013) *School of Kingdom Ministry Manual*. Coaching Saints Publications. p.133. (Permission granted)
[5] The four steps are taken from Bethel Sozo.

is it return to, in other words we turn back towards, we once again head in the right direction. However, the term repentance also refers to having a changing of mind. Therefore, when we repent of believing the lie, we are literally changing our mind as to what we believe about who we are and we return back to the truth of what we should believe.

Forgive

Secondly, we need to forgive the person(s) who may have spoken those lies over us; those people who have, maybe unconsciously, placed those labels over us. I have found as I have spoken to people and ministered to them through a Sozo session that forgiveness is a key to freedom. It's the key to unlocking the prison we have been living in for years. The good news is that the key is in our hands, it is our choice if we want to use the key and forgive them.

Unforgiveness hurts us more than we realise. It often causes us to have bitterness, resentment and anger towards the one who hurt us in the first place. We agree with the lie that we are hurting the person as an act of revenge. We, however, are the one that drink the poison of that bitterness etc. We are the ones who find ourselves locked in these prisons of false identity. The writer of Hebrews says there should be no bitter root growing (Hebrews 12:15). However, we are the ones who get to decide if we want to forgive and thus begin to unlock the prison gates. Forgiveness is a choice not a feeling. There is a misconception that forgiving someone makes light of the wrong action. True forgiveness means you are free from the burden you are carrying and you are able to move aside and allow God to choose to deal with the one who hurt you, how

He pleases. True forgiveness is to never remind that person of what they have done.

Reject the Lie

This means that we choose to change our view point, we choose to no longer partner with the lying tongue of the enemy. We need to reject the lies that have been spoken over us, reject the labels we have been carrying. We need to recognise the lie we have believed about ourselves and declare the truth of what the Bible says about us, we need to begin to look at how the Father sees us and agree with His thoughts.

"The tongue has the power of life and death, and those who love it will eat its fruit."

Proverbs 18:21

What we say produces either life or death; we have the power to speak life into our souls and spirits. Our declarations of the truth will begin to bring about a changed mind, as we declare the truth we will begin to reject the lie. Just as light and darkness cannot coexist (2 Corinthians 6:14), either there is darkness or there is light, similarly lies and truth cannot exist in the same place. It is impossible for the lie that 'we will never amount to anything' to exist in the same space as the truth that He knows the plans for my life, His plans that are good, plans that will give us a hope and a future (Jeremiah 29:11). Either one is true and not the other. They cannot both be true, and so as we begin to reject the lie the truth will begin to grow inside of us.

Accept the Truth

After we have chosen to release forgiveness to those who have spoken those lies over us and we have rejected that lie and declared the truth, so we can begin to accept the truth. We cannot accept the truth until we have rejected the lie in the first place. How do we accept it? Aside from declaring the truth, we can begin to walk in the truth. It might be that we don't feel it, it might be a challenge to even say it out loud but as we persevere and change our thinking patterns, and maybe even change our actions, we will begin to accept the truths. The lies we have believed, the labels that people have put on us have not happened overnight, over a period of time as we repeatedly heard the lie, we have begun to partner with it and so it will be with the truth. As we daily reject the lie and declare the truth out loud, we will begin to change our thoughts patterns. Over time the lie will begin to lose its control over us, and the truth will begin to take root in our hearts.

"Then you will know the truth, and the truth will set you free."

John 8:32

Whilst the key to the prison is forgiveness, so is the rejection of the lie and acceptance of the truth the way to opening the prison door and walking free.

Growing in our true identity is a journey or a process; it is something that comes by revelation. As we embark upon this journey and as we seek to discover the truth of who we are, as the Father begins to bring that revelation by His Spirit, we begin to overwrite our former programming, our wrong way of thinking and we begin to be restored to our original programming, our true DNA.

Our wrong way of thinking is not how we were created; we were not designed with false labels over us. We have been tainted by sin and lost our true identity. But all is not lost if we are willing to go on this journey and I believe as you are reading this book, then you have already begun to travel that journey, our true identity can be restored.

As Leif Hetland put it:

> *When your true identity is revealed, then everything will change. You suddenly have access to the business empire built by your Dad, and your life will never be the same.* [6]

When we have a true and right understanding of our identity as children of God and what that means, then we can begin to move from the prison we find ourselves in, into the freedom that He always intended for His children. Our life will literally never be the same again in a truly amazing new way.

The real answer to the question "what is my identity?" is found as we become immersed in love. Our real identity is not in what we do for a living, or how good we are in life, at work, at home, it is not how high we climb up the social ladder. Our real identity is only found when we know our Heavenly Father and experience the love He has for us. Our true identity is found in Him.

Prayer:

Father today I recognise that I have been living under a false identity. I repent of partnering with that lie and I choose to forgive those who have spoken over my life any wrong or negative words and I reject the thoughts

---

[6] Hetland, L. (2013) *Baptism of Love*. Self-published by Leif Hetland p.43. (Permission granted)

that don't line up with what You say. I choose to accept the truth that You have given me my identity, You are the One who knows who I am. Today I choose to listen to Your voice.

Mark Russell

Forgiven

Throughout my life, more especially whilst I have had the privilege of living in Malawi, I have come across people who have asked the question "Am I forgiven?" It is common in Malawi to have an incomplete understanding of our forgiveness. Some people may think that not all their sins are forgiven. Others may think if we sin we lose our salvation. Through this incomplete understanding these people may wrongly think that Father God is expecting perfect people. It is as though the sacrifice of Jesus was not sufficient, or worse, that the death and resurrection was not actually for them at all. This in effect nullifies the complete work of Jesus on the cross. Consequently, they turn grace into something that it is not. Grace becomes works, as though it is something that is earned rather than something that is freely given.

It is common for the enemy to try and cause us to think that our sins will not be forgiven, to try and convince us that this time we have 'blown it' and we have now removed ourselves from the grace of Jesus. He causes us to remember times when we did something wrong and as we dwell on these things I believe two things happen. Firstly, we take our eyes off Jesus by focusing on our past mistakes. This ultimately puts more attention on the devil, which of course is where he wants us to focus. When we do that we begin to empower him, we begin to see more and more our own failings, rather than see who we really are and who we really represent. Secondly, we focus on our own sinfulness and are reminded of how much we have done wrong, we might begin to question our salvation and indeed the forgiveness of Jesus. It is interesting how these same people may be happy to extend forgiveness to others, but when it comes to their own wrongdoing, they just appear to see their own dirty rags. They see what they have done wrong rather than see themselves through the blood of Jesus, which is exactly how God sees each one of us. When the Father looks at us, He does not see the dirty rags, He sees us washed by the blood of Jesus. We need to begin to see ourselves as Father God sees us, it is time we opened our eyes to the truth of the power of the cross. It is time we understood exactly what He has done for us; that the work of the cross is totally sufficient and there is nothing more Jesus needs to do.

If we have repented of a sin and have asked for Father's forgiveness and the enemy reminds us of that sin, Father says "What sin? I have no idea what you are talking about". His grace is endless; His mercies are new each day. Not only has He forgiven our sins He has also forgotten it; it is no longer in the mind of God anymore.

> *"as far as the east is from the west, so far has He removed our transgression from us"*
>
> *Psalm 103:12*

The sin we have committed no longer affects our relationship with Him. In fact they will never again be mentioned by our Heavenly Father. Our sin is so far removed from us it is like it is no longer seen by Him because of the blood of Jesus. Matthew Henry suggests that God chooses not to remember what we have done.[1] You cannot be forgiven for what you haven't done, in Him it is like we have not committed that sin. It is gone forever!

If God has forgotten it, why haven't we?

When we dwell on our mistakes it does not give glory to God, in fact it dishonours Him. Why? Because we stop seeing ourselves as who we truly are and instead we begin to focus on our old self. By dwelling on our former identity we stop recognising the work of Jesus, we stop living in the royal robes we have been given and we begin once again to live in the rags which we have supposedly left behind at the cross.

If I stop wearing my wedding ring and act as though I am not married, the truth does not change that I am still married. But acting in that manner dishonours my wife and discredits the vows I said to her before God. Choosing to live as though we are not forgiven does not change the fact we are forgiven. Just as I want to honour my wedding vows and choose to live as though I am married, so we also should choose to live in the truth that we are forgiven. Living as though we are not forgiven dishonours what Jesus accomplished on the cross.

What does the Bible say?

---

[1] *Blue Letter Bible*. Available at: https://www.blueletterbible.org/Comm/mhc/Psa/Psa_103.cfm?a=581012 (Accessed: 25th April 2020).

"In the same way, count yourselves dead to sin, but alive to God in Christ Jesus."

Romans 6:11

Paul seems very clear here; if we are washed in the blood of Jesus then we are dead to sin. We are now wearing royal robes and not dirty rags. Sin has been put to death. We are free! Free from the old way of life, free from the bondages that ensnared us, free from guilt and shame. The good news is the blood of Jesus has wiped out the power of sin over our lives, it has been crucified, it has no power over us and therefore we are free.

"We died to sin; how can we live in it any longer? Or don't you know that all of us who were baptised into Christ Jesus were baptised into His death? We were therefore buried with Him through baptism into death in order that, just as Christ was raised from the dead through the glory of the Father, we too may live a new life. If we have been united with Him like this in His death, we will certainly also be united with Him in His resurrection. For we know that our old self was crucified with Him so that the body of sin might be done away with, **that we should no longer be slaves to sin** *– because anyone who has died has been freed from sin."*

Romans 6:2b-7 (emphasis added)

As Paul says in verse 7 we should no longer be slaves to sin. In other words we no longer have to look back; we no longer have to look at our sins. A slave is only free when he is no longer under the influence of his master. We are no longer under the influence of our old master, sin.

"For sin shall not be your master, because you are not under law, but under grace."

Romans 6:14

We are under grace therefore we are free. Just as a freed slave does not look back but looks forward, so we too must look forward. An athlete runs his fastest when he is looking forward, if he looks back to see the competition behind him, he slows down and is in danger of tripping and falling. When we continually look back at our old life, we also are in danger of falling back into our old way of life and become in danger of discrediting the cross.

We have all made mistakes, we have all done things wrong, but that is the point, that was then, that was the past. The fact is that we will still make mistakes and therefore all our future sins are covered by the blood of Jesus.

"If we confess our sins, He is faithful and just and will forgive us our sins and purify us from all unrighteousness."

1 John 1:9

When we read this verse it seems quite clear that all that is required is a confession, which is to admit your mistake. What happens when we confess? Again John leaves us in no doubt, God is faithful and God is just and we are forgiven, we are purified of all our wrong doing. More than that we are made righteous, meaning that what we did has been put right, we are now in a right place with our Father. Nothing in this passage suggests that there is any question over what will happen. There are no limits; it appears that **every time** we confess then **every time** we are forgiven. No question, there are no ifs or buts. It is fact, we are forgiven. We must actively receive this forgiveness, this means to live as though this is true. You might find it helpful to declare that you are forgiven.

Repentance is more than a way to bypass hell, it is more than a get out of jail free card, it is the way into a relationship with God. At the point of repentance we become children of God and consequently we are able to freely enter into the relationship He promised and a life of freedom with Him.

We need to understand being forgiven is who we are. Just as I am a husband and just as I am a son, so too I am forgiven. I will never stop being a son, and in the same way I will never stop being forgiven, it is part of my identity, it is part of who I am.

> *"In Him we have redemption through His blood, the forgiveness of sins in accordance with the riches of God's grace."*
>
> *Ephesians 1:7*

Every Christian is forgiven; forgiveness has been freely given us because of the blood. Sins can only be washed away; sins can only be forgiven through the shedding of blood. Because of the blood of Jesus we are forgiven, no more blood sacrifice is required, no-one else's blood, it is only 'in Him', in His blood that we can find forgiveness.

> *"In fact the law requires that nearly everything be cleansed with blood, and without blood there is no forgiveness."*
>
> *Hebrews 9:22*

The blood that is talked about here is the blood of Jesus. The blood that was spilled is always enough to bring total and complete forgiveness. Jesus said "It is finished" (John 19:30) meaning that all He came to do was now completed. There was nothing left outstanding, the job was done, the task was complete and His assignment was finished. The writer of Hebrews uses the term "He sat down" four times.[2] When someone sits down it suggests that there is nothing more that can be done; Jesus sat down for exactly that reason, there was nothing more that could be done. He had done, once and for all, everything that was required. Nothing else is required for our forgiveness. If there was, then surely the work of Christ would not be complete, surely God was just cruel to send His Son to die. Surely it was a pointless act?

However, the verse we looked at in Ephesians 1:7 also shows us it is in accordance with the riches of God's grace. Grace is a gift, it is not earned, it is not a reward for doing well. It is something we receive because the Giver wants to bless us. The Father loves us so much, He wants to bless us so much, that He has given us this free gift. It is ours for the taking; all we have to do is accept it. If a friend invites me on an all-expenses paid trip abroad it would be rude, if not offensive, to suggest that I pay my own way. All of our debts have already been paid; we are no longer required to pay. Jesus has paid in full. Or to put it another way if a friend invites me over for dinner, it would be foolish, if not rude of me to eat beforehand and not eat with the friend who invited me. We have been invited out for dinner; we have been invited to eat of the free meal of forgiveness.

---

[2] Hebrews 1:3; Hebrews 8:1; Hebrews 10:12; and Hebrews 12:2

> *"For it is by grace you have been saved, through faith – and this not from yourselves, it is the gift of God – not by works so that no one can boast."*
>
> *Ephesians 2:8-9*

We cannot boast to others about how good we have been, we are unable to truthfully say our salvation is our own because of this good deed or that good act. No! Just as the meal was cooked by my friend, so I cannot take any credit for it. So too is the free gift of salvation and forgiveness, it is a gift given by God so that no man can boast.

God has so much grace to pour out on each of us, there is never a shortfall. His grace is always overflowing, the more He pours out the more there is to be poured out.

Mark Gyde in his book 'A Father to You' says:

> *"in the church today there are many spiritual orphans - people who know their sins are forgiven but constantly try to earn God's favour through their own effort."* [3]

No matter how hard we try we cannot earn God's favour or forgiveness. The love the Father has for us is a message of grace and there is nothing we can do that will make God love us any more. Similarly, if we live under a cloud of guilt we are no less loved!

Maybe you have said something along the lines of "If you forgive me of this sin then I'll do something in return." It is as if we are trying to twist God's arm. It is like we are trying to persuade Him. With this thought process we are misunderstanding His nature and His heart towards us. It

---

[3] Gyde, M. (2011) *A Father to You.* p.40. (Permission granted)

highlights something about our own motives and trying to obtain something we cannot do in the first place. Maybe we think we will feel better about ourselves without feeling bad about what we have done. However, we cannot twist God's arm. We can see His hand of forgiveness. We can live like forgiven people. We can live under the true grace He has for us, and not sometimes our false understanding of grace. We need to live in the truth of the words of Paul that it is a free gift. (Ephesians 2:9). All these truths would be enjoyed if we truly understood God's nature and if we wanted genuine relationship.

You might be thinking 'If you knew how badly I have messed up,' my response would be 'He *does* know, yet the grace of God still stands.' There are no exceptions, there are no exclusions. I don't need to know how badly you have messed up; you just need to know God says

"My grace is sufficient for you"

2 Corinthians 12:9

You see His grace is sufficient. His grace is all we need. There is nothing else that is required. The book of Lamentations says:

"His mercies are new every morning"

Lamentations 3:23

Each morning we wake up we can be assured that today we receive new mercies. They are from the same Source, but they are new for today.

This being said, let us remember Paul's teaching to the Romans:

> *"What shall we say then? Shall we go on sinning so that grace may increase? By no means! We died to sin, how can we live in it any longer?"*
>
> *Romans 6:1-2*

The grace of God is so great, it is never ending, we can never out sin His grace. There is no limit to the amount of grace that can be given to each one of us; it is always available. His grace empowers us not to sin in the first place. Notice Paul says "Shall we go on sinning so that grace may increase?" The grace that is given, whilst free, is not an excuse to carry on sinning. Paul reminds us we are now dead to sin and it no longer has mastery over us, therefore we are able to no longer live in it. I appreciate that many of us constantly feel bound by the same cycle of sin. We all struggle with sin, but as we shall see in the chapter relating to royalty, we are no longer sinners. We need to recognise how Father sees us as forgiven. He sees us as though we have not sinned. Sin is no longer in our nature; sin is no longer in our identity. Though we may sin, we are not sinners.

I used the example earlier of being married. I know my wife loves me, she loves me unconditionally and because of that I want to do all I can to extend that love back to her. Each day she continues to love me and so each day I do all I can to show her my love. It is not for me to take for granted the love she has for me and so act how I want and have a disregard for that love. I am a married man and I live as such. I am in essence dead to the single life; I have given my life to love my wife as best I can. And so it is with our life in Jesus, we have received the grace required, and as a result we want do to all we can to respect that. We do all we can to show our gratitude to Him, not by deliberately sinning, but by living under the grace that He has freely given us.

It is no good buying a brand new car but continuing to drive the old decrepit one with the new car kept in the garage. Why would we live as though we have not paid and purchased the new car? We have a new life, so why do we live as though we are part of the old life; Jesus has paid for us, He purchased our new life. It is time we lived in that truth.

Unforgivable sin

During my time in Malawi whilst I was teaching on the subject of forgiveness and how each one of us is always forgiven because of the grace of God, I was asked the question, what about the sin against the Holy Spirit? If I sin against the Holy Spirit am I not forgiven? Those who asked this question were living in fear that they might not be forgiven just in case they had sinned against the Holy Spirit.

So what is the unforgivable sin?

Paul in his letter to the Ephesians says:

"And do not grieve the Holy Spirit of God, with whom you were sealed for the day of redemption"

Ephesians 4:30

The Holy Spirit has been given to us for the day of redemption; He has been given to us because we have been delivered from sin. We are redeemed; we are made right with God, through the blood of Jesus. So if the Holy Spirit, has been given to us because we are forgiven, how can we grieve Him?

Let us take a look at what Jesus says:

> *"I tell you the truth, all the sins and blasphemes of men will be forgiven them. But whoever blasphemes the Holy Spirit will never be forgiven; he is guilty of an eternal sin."*
>
> *Mark 3:28-29*

The word grieve in Ephesians 4:30 could also mean to offend,[4] therefore Paul is instructing us not to offend the Holy Spirit. Jesus also instructs us not to blaspheme the Holy Spirit. To blaspheme the Holy Spirit is to deny the power of God and so it seems that grieving the Holy Spirit could be a step towards blaspheming the Holy Spirit. This passage in Mark could be seen to be quite a harsh one. On the face of it we are reading that if we commit this sin of blaspheming the Holy Spirit then we are guilty of an eternal sin which cannot be forgiven. We read passages such as the one we looked at earlier from 1 John:

> *"If we confess our sins, He is faithful and just and will forgive us our sins and purify us from all unrighteousness."*
>
> *1 John 1:9*

The two passages appear not to reconcile with each other. On the one hand if we confess our sin we are forgiven, yet on the other we are told there is one sin, no matter if we confess it or not, that will never be forgiven.

How are we to live in the freedom of being forgiven? How can forgiveness be part of who we are if there is a sin that we will not be forgiven of? How can grace be grace if it does not extend to all sins? Maybe we have committed the eternal sin?

---

[4] *Blue Letter Bible.* Available at: https://www.blueletterbible.org/lang/lexicon/lexicon.cfm?Strongs=G3076&t=NIV (Accessed 25th April 2020).

In order to answer this more fully and show us that all I have said previously on the subject of forgiveness still holds true, we need to look more at what the work of the Holy Spirit is:

"All this I have spoken while still with you. But the counsellor, the Holy Spirit, whom the Father will send in my name, will teach you all things and remind you of everything I have said to you."

John 14:25-26

Firstly, the Holy Spirt will remind us of all the things Jesus has said to us, as Jesus is the Truth, He reminds us of the truth.

Later in the same gospel we read:

"Unless I go away, the Counsellor will not come to you; but I go, I will send Him to you. When He comes, He will convict the world of guilt in regard to sin and righteousness and judgement: In regard to sin, because men do not believe in Me; in regards to righteousness, because I am going to the Father, where you will see Me no longer, and in regard to judgement, because the prince of this world now stands condemned."

John 16:7-11

In this passage we read that the work of the Holy Spirt is to convict the world of sin. Why? Jesus says because men do not believe in Him.

So the work of the Holy Spirit is to remind us of all that Jesus has said, to remind us of the truths that Jesus spoke and to convict us of sin, because men do not believe in Jesus. The work of the Holy Spirit is to point us to our immense need for Jesus. He points us to the work of Jesus on the cross and the grace supplied in that act. Therefore it could be said that the unforgivable sin, the sin against the Holy Spirit is to ignore the work of the Spirit, and therefore deny that Jesus died for each one of us. So to sin against the Holy Spirit is to reject Jesus, and we know that Jesus is the only way to the Father. Therefore, rejecting Jesus is to reject the free forgiveness and life that He brings, which ultimately will never be forgiven.

As a result, if we believe in Jesus, it is impossible for us to commit the unforgivable sin. Therefore all that has been said in this chapter still stands, we are forgiven, it is who we are, it is part of our identity, and if we are forgiven then we are dead to sin. We can be assured that forgiveness is ours and our sin can never take that from us.

There is nothing that can separate us from Jesus. There is nothing that if we believe in Jesus, we cannot be forgiven of. We read again in Romans:

"For I am convinced that neither death nor life, neither angels nor demons, neither the present nor the future, nor any powers, neither height nor depth, nor anything else in all creation, will be able to separate us from the love of God that is in Christ Jesus our Lord"

Romans 8:38-39

This is a long list; a complete list that demonstrates how much God has invested His life in us. He will not allow anything to come between Him and His children, there is nothing He will allow to come between Him and us, even death! In fact Paul says to emphasise the point "nor anything else in all creation". If we were unsure before, there should now be no question in our minds, there is nothing! However, Bill Johnson in his book 'The Supernatural Power of a Transformed Mind' suggests there is one thing not mentioned and that is the past. He says:

> *'It is our past that can separate us from an awareness of the love of God, if we let it become our present identity.'* [5]

Notice it is just the awareness and not the actual love of God that our past can separate us from. It is therefore the awareness of the forgiveness of God, in no way does it separate us from His actual forgiveness.

We have come full circle; part of our identity is the fact we are forgiven. But so often we listen to the devil reminding us of our past and this robs us of who we really are and it robs us of our awareness of the love of God. As a result we become focused on the very things we have done wrong, and in turn we lose the sense of the mighty work of the cross, and the forgiveness that is ours through Jesus.

It is time that we live in the freedom that Jesus bought us. It is time to live in the freedom of our forgiveness and not dwell on what we have done, or even dwell on what we might do. It is time to take the focus away from the one who wants to keep us from the truth. It is time to look to who Jesus has made us, forgiven people, and in doing so glorifying His name. It is time we wear the royal robes He has given us and leave the old dirty rags where they belong, at the foot of the cross.

Prayer:

Jesus I thank You for the total forgiveness You have given to me. I thank You that Your grace is sufficient for me. I thank You that You alone have bought my freedom, and so I no longer have to dwell on my past because You only see my future.

---

[5] Johnson, B. (2005), *The Supernatural Power of a Transformed Mind*. Destiny Image. p.111. (Permission granted)

Mark Russell

Made in the Image of God

"Then God said, "Let us make mankind in our image, in our likeness, so that they may rule over the fish in the sea and the birds in the sky, over the livestock and all the wild animals, and over all the creatures that move along the ground." So God created mankind in His own image, in the image of God He created them; male and female He created them."

Genesis 1:26-28

In the UK coins and bank notes all have an image of the Queen's head; we all recognise this is the Queen. So it is with the Father, we are made in His image and consequently there is an impression of Him on our lives; people recognise God in us.

When we look in a mirror we see a reflection of our self. Because we are made in the image of God we can see an image of the Father. Therefore, what we see is a representation of ourselves but also an image of Father God in us.

This is also true of how people see us even though they may not recognise it. When people look at you or I, they see a reflection of the Father. Have you ever heard someone say "what is different about you?" The difference is the reflection of Father. They see something of Him in you.

When a new born baby first comes into world people say "he has your eyes" or "she is just like her dad", we see something of the parent in the child. So it is with God, we have been made in His likeness, in His image; therefore we have all the attributes of Him in us, everything that He is so we are. In other words the attributes of God: love, goodness, kindness (the list is extensive), we too share those same attributes. We have the ability to love, to exhibit His goodness and to be kind. I will look later in the chapter at some of these attributes.

The writer of Hebrews describes Jesus as:

"The Son is the radiance of God's glory and the exact representation of His being, sustaining all things by His powerful word."

Hebrews 1:3

Just as Jesus the Son of God is the exact representation of His Father, so too are we as children of God, a representation of our Father. We carry the Holy Spirit, we carry the very presence of God, therefore when people look at us they see a difference, they see something of God. They might see His love, His mercy, His faithfulness.

The Hebrew root of the Latin phrase for image of God—*imago Dei*—means image, shadow or likeness of God[1]. We are a

---

[1] *Blue Letter Bible*. Available at:
https://www.blueletterbible.org/lexicon/h6754/niv/wlc/0-1/ (Accessed 5th

snapshot or copy of God. What is God like? We only need to look in the mirror, what we should see in us is the nature of what God is like. By being made in His image we carry something of the presence of Him in us, we are a copy or shadow of Him, we are a *true* likeness of who He is. Therefore, we can and should be able to represent Him here on earth.

The words used in Genesis 1:26-27, "image" (tselem) and "likeness" (demuth) in the Hebrew mean something that resembles or similar to.[2] Therefore Genesis 1:26 suggests that we are made like Him and resemble Him. To be made in the image of God means we are recognised as a representation of Him, in other words for us as believers those around us do not just see us, they see something of Father too.[3]

We are not just like Him, yes we have His characteristics, we have His attributes, and we have the ability to love and show kindness, but we are also to represent Him. We are able to represent Him because we are like Him. In John's first letter we read:

> *"In this way, love is made complete among us so that we will have confidence on the day of judgement,* **because in this world we are like Him.***"*
>
> 1 John 4:17 *(emphasis added)*

April 2021)
[2] *Blue Letter Bible*. Available at: https://www.blueletterbible.org/search/dictionary/viewtopic.cfm?topic=IT0 003852 (Accessed 25th April 2021)
[3] Puttman, R. (2013) *School of Kingdom Ministry Manual*. Coaching Saints Publications. p.83.(Permission granted)

We are the likeness of Him in both nature and character. Consequently everything that Jesus is and was on this earth is true for you and I. We are like Him, our nature is like His and so too is our character. Therefore just as Jesus is love, so we are love in this world. We are called to demonstrate that love to our friends, family, neighbours and work colleagues. Jesus was peace and so we are not only able to have that peace ourselves, but also carry peace to those around us who are in need of it. We are to be His hands and His feet to the people we meet. Have you heard the phrase "What would Jesus do?" It is time to truly ask that question of ourselves. It is time to understand that being made in His image is more than just a nice verse in the Bible or more than a description of who we are; we are indeed to be Jesus to those around us. We are called to love like He loves, we are called to show mercy like He shows mercy. In order for people to see Jesus in us then we must demonstrate and represent Jesus in our lives. As we represent Jesus in our lives people don't just see us or our good works but additionally they see something of Jesus, they see something of His character shining through us.

This gives us hope. Perhaps you may have felt overwhelmed that we have to be Jesus, we have to represent Jesus to those around us? Maybe you feel you couldn't do that, you are aware of your own failings. But look closer, "in relationship with God and each other." All we do we should do out of relationship with Him. Father desires relationship with us. Not a relationship where we just come to Him with our burdens and tell Him our concerns, or our 'shopping list' of things we want Him to do. But a relationship where we also acknowledge Him; being quiet and allowing Him to speak. Listening to Him about what He thinks about us, for Him to love on us.

What kind of relationship would I have with my wife if I only ever asked her to do this or that? If I didn't allow time for her to speak to me, but more than that, for me to demonstrate my love for her too?

I remember a time I was driving to work and I asked God "What do You expect of me today?" I was shocked by the answer He gave me. He said "I expect nothing of you." He continued to say "If I expect something of you, then you would have the ability to fail me." Father showed me that we cannot fail Him, we can never disappoint Him. I was able to go to work that day in the freedom that He expects nothing of me; I was to just be me. I did not have to manufacture anything or look for opportunities to be Jesus. I was simply free to be Jesus, free to represent Jesus to those around me. I remember walking in that newly found freedom and having the most amazing God centred conversation about Jesus with my entire office. I had the opportunity to talk about the amazing grace found in Him to a Muslim colleague. I was able to represent something of Jesus in the knowledge and freedom of Him having no expectations of me. I am certain that had I not had that freedom, I would have indeed either missed any opportunity or done something out of my own efforts. I was able to represent Jesus out of a relationship with Him, in partnership with Him, rather than any false understanding that I had to do anything.

Paul writes in 1 Corinthians:

> *"... man is the image and glory of God."*
>
> *1 Corinthians 11:7b*

Paul seems to suggest that being made in His image is not something we can own as a physical thing, it is not a functional thing, but more it is a state of being, it is a gift from God. Being made in the image of God is our identity, it is who we are.

Many people try to change the way they look, it is like they want to become someone else. They see something in others and think I want to be like them rather than seeing them as God sees them. The truth is they are made in the image of God. Is God perfect? Yes. Did God say when referring to the creation of mankind "It is very good?" Yes. If we are made in His image and if God looked at us and thought that, then why do we try and alter what has been made very good by the perfect Creator? Why do we see ourselves as something other than perfect? Why do we see ourselves in a way that says I am not happy with what I see? We need to have the revelation of who we are, we need to have the revelation of the truth that we are made in His image, the very image of God. This image, as I said earlier is a copy.

How do we represent God?

As we have seen this gift is not simply functional; there is a purpose to it. To be in the image of God is to represent God and to demonstrate something of His nature and character to those around us. Just before we look God's characteristics and nature, let us first read two passages:

"For in the image of God has God made mankind"

Genesis 9:6

> *"With the tongue we praise our Lord and Father, and with it we curse men, who have been made in God's likeness."*
>
> *James 3:9*

If we are a representation of God, then we are like Him. The passage in Genesis 9 says we have been made in the image of God. If we are made in His image, it stands to reason there is an explanation as to why. In the verse in James we read that we are made in God's likeness, meaning that we are like God, therefore surely we are to be like Him on earth. We are to represent Him. We have inherited His nature, His character and His attributes. Just as I have inherited some of my dad's attributes, so we have our Heavenly Father's attributes, therefore we can be like Him on earth.

Paul teaches that the qualities of God or the nature of God have been seen through His creation, and since we are made in His image and represent Him, I believe this incorporates the creation of mankind.

> *"For since the creation of the world God's invisible qualities – His eternal power and divine nature – have been clearly seen, being understood from what has been made, so that men are without excuse."*
>
> *Romans 1:20*

It seems clear that God Himself chooses to demonstrate something of Himself through His very creation, including through you and I. It appears that our mandate is to represent the Father. Having understood that we are to represent God because we are made in His image, let us now look at God and see that what He is like.

God is Good

> *"Taste and see that the LORD is good"*
>
> *Psalm 34:8a*

We are encouraged here to taste and see His goodness, or as The Passion Translation says "Drink deeply the pleasure of God. Experience for yourself the joyous mercies He gives." It seems that His goodness can be experienced; it is not something that is far out of our reach. His goodness is so close we can experience it; we can taste it.

As we experience His goodness, so we then can begin to understand. Experience leads to understanding. Just as if you were to eat a strawberry, that experience would lead you to understand something of its sweetness.

When we both experience and understand His goodness, then our perception of Him begins to change, and so we are able to see our situations through the lens of His goodness, and not through the lens of our earthly understanding of what we think His goodness is like.

I am sure like me you may have questioned His goodness in certain situations, or maybe people have questioned you about His goodness. The apostle Paul says:

> *"We are afflicted in every way, but not crushed; perplexed, but not driven to despair; persecuted, but not forsaken; struck down, but not destroyed; always carrying in the body the death of Jesus, so that the life of Jesus may also be manifested in our bodies."*
>
> *2 Corinthians 4:8–10 (ESV)*

Although Paul is saying we face troubles, we also know from his letter to the Philippians that he is content (Philippians 4:11). Paul still understands that God is greater; He is bigger than everything you and I will ever face. What we face should lead us to look more towards Him and see Him in it.

Even when we don't "feel it" we are able to stand on the rock of His goodness. We read in Psalms

> *"Surely goodness and love shall follow me all the days of my life…"*
>
> *Psalm 23:6*

This verse paints a picture of His goodness pursuing us. I am sure we have seen nature programmes where an animal is hunting. In that moment the animal is not distracted, nothing will cause it to take its eyes off what it has spotted, it remains entirely focused. The animal will chase it down; it will run hard after it. Unlike the animal which will give up when that which it sought out, eludes its hunter, Father will never give up. We can never outrun His goodness towards us.

We can quickly forget this truth when our circumstances do not line up with our understanding of the goodness of God. We should not let our circumstances change our understanding of His goodness, but rather we should let His goodness change our understanding of our circumstances.

The goodness of God is not at the mercy of our circumstances, it is rooted in His eternal nature.

It is the cross where we can ultimately see the goodness of God. It is in the victory of the death and the resurrection of Jesus that we can see the magnitude of His goodness towards each of us.

"Give thanks to the LORD, for he is good; his love endures forever."

Psalm 107:1

So how can we demonstrate this goodness to others?

Paul in Galatians tell us that the fruit of the Spirit is goodness (Galatians 5:22). As the Spirit lives in us we have the fruit of goodness growing inside each of us and as a result we can demonstrate His goodness. As we experience more of His goodness, and as we allow His Spirit to permeate us, so we are able to allow that same goodness to emanate from us and show goodness to others.

God is Kind

What does it mean to be kind? The Collins dictionary uses words such as being helpful or being considerate. It is easy to be kind to someone if we receive the same back. If someone is considerate toward us, then we find it easier to be considerate back to them.

I believe, however, that the kindness of God is different to the kindness of man. His kindness is not dictated by our actions. We know the bible teaches that even though we were separated from God, He still bridged that divide and made it possible for us to come back into relationship with Him (Romans 6-8).

God has shown us His kindness through Jesus.

"so that in the coming ages He might show the immeasurable riches of His grace in kindness toward us in Christ Jesus."

Ephesians 2:7

The cross is the heart of His kindness towards us. Our rebellion and sin caused us to be alienated from God, without hope and without life. God's kindness meant Jesus was sacrificed and subsequently experienced the worst of human rejection and punishment in order that he could destroy the things that would destroy us.

> *"But He was pierced for our transgressions, He was crushed for our iniquities; the punishment that brought us peace was on Him, and by His wounds we are healed."*
>
> *Isaiah 53:5*

It is at the cross we can see the kindness of God. Kindness is part of the nature of God because He will give to us even if we do not give back to Him. In other words, His actions are not dependent upon us.

Let's have a look at the story of King David and God's kindness demonstrated in his life:

> *"the war between the house of Saul and the house of David lasted a long time. David grew stronger and stronger, while the house of Saul grew weaker and weaker."*
>
> *2 Samuel 3:1*

We can see from this verse that there was no love lost between Saul and David. You would imagine that when one of your oldest enemy dies, after all this time, you would celebrate. However, David has a completely different response. David mourns, weeps, and fasts for both Saul and his son (David's friend) Jonathan.

> *"Then David and all the men with him took hold of their clothes and tore them. They mourned and wept and fasted till evening for Saul and his son Jonathan, and for the army of the Lord and for the nation of Israel, because they had fallen by the sword."*
>
> *2 Samuel 1:11-12*

This is a remarkable response to the death of your enemy; David is now able to be crowned King. More than that, he orders the man who brought the news that he had killed Saul to be killed. (2 Samuel 1:14-15). In other words, although David was at war with Saul, he did not want to be linked to Saul's death and would not reward such an act.

David was a man who experienced something of the kindness of God; he recognised that God has a different viewpoint to man. All this before he truly understood what it was to receive God's kindness. Yet David knew there was a difference between the kindness of man and the kindness of God. In 2 Samuel 9 we read:

> *"The king asked, "Is there no one still alive from the house of Saul to whom I can show* **God's kindness**?""*
>
> *2 Samuel 9:3 (emphasis added)*

The way in which David reacts, I think, is very different to the way most of us would react. David recognised that in order to show the kindness of God, you act towards others in a way in which it does not depend on a response from the other. You treat the other in a positive light even if you know they will not treat you the same way.

With all that we have read, and remembering that the ultimate act of kindness is at the cross and that God's kindness leads us to repentance (Romans 2:4), we should be encouraged to act in the same way, to demonstrate the kindness of Father to others.

As we are made in the image of God, we have the capacity to show that same kindness to others. We are to be kind to others even if we have not received the same. Paul teaches in Ephesians

"Be kind and compassionate to one another, forgiving each other, just as in Christ God forgave you."

Ephesians 4:32

We are to demonstrate His kindness by reflecting the heart of the Father.

God is Loving

"God is love"

1 John 4:8

I am sure we all understand the truth that God is love, but equally I am sure at times we find it difficult to experience His love. However, His love is to be experienced. Just as I experience the love my wife has for me, so too are we created to experience Father's love for us. Paul prays for us in his letter to the Ephesians:

…"that you being rooted and established in love, that may have power with all the saints, to grasp how wide and long and high and deep is the love of Christ, and to know His love which surpasses knowledge…."

Ephesians 3:17-19

Paul is praying that we would comprehend and grasp the magnitude of His love for us.

What does it mean for God to be love? We read in John's gospel one of the most well known verses in the bible:

"For God so loved the world that He gave His one and only son"

John 3:16

The love the Father has for each one of us is so great that He sacrificed His only Son. He allowed His Son, more than that, He sent His Son to demonstrate the love He has for each of us. John continues later in his Gospel:

"Greater love has no one than this, that he lay down His life for His friends."

John 15:13

Why would anyone make such a monumental sacrifice if it was not to be experienced? When we experience something we feel it or we are touched by it. Imagine if someone saved your life, what would your reaction be? You would be very grateful. You would most likely want to demonstrate your gratitude in some way. The love He has is so great that He lavishes His love upon us (1 John 3:1). The feeling of love that He has for each of us is almost beyond words. He is in love with us. His love is not to give us a nice feeling, but rather we are to be affected by it; His love is so strong that we are to be transformed by it.

As we are transformed by His love, it compels us to love back. The love of the Father demands a response. What is that response? Simply that we love others, that we demonstrate the love we have received to others.

> *"We love because he first loved us."*
>
> 1 John 4:19

Prayer:

Father I thank You that I am created in Your image and that means I can represent You here on earth. I thank You that I can be Your hands and feet. Father, as I demonstrate something of who You are within my sphere of influence, among my friends and family, may I give You all the glory.

Mark Russell

Co-heirs with Christ

"The Spirit you received does not make you slaves, so that you live in fear again; rather, the Spirit you received brought about your adoption to sonship. And by Him we cry, "Abba, Father." The Spirit Himself testifies with our spirit that we are God's children. Now if we are children, then we are heirs—heirs of God and co-heirs with Christ, if indeed we share in His sufferings in order that we may also share in His glory."

Romans 8:15-17

"So you are no longer a slave, but God's child; and since you are His child, God has made you also an heir."

Galatians 4:7

We are co-heirs with Christ

"so that, having been justified by His grace, we might become heirs having the hope of eternal life."

Titus 3:7

There are many blessings for us as believers to be heirs with Christ. However, I only began to gain real understanding and revelation a few years ago when Father began to speak to me about who I am. The concept of an heir is commonly understood. We understand an heir to be someone who can legally make a claim to another person's possessions upon that person's death. In the UK we have a monarchy; the Queen is the head and her heir is her son, Prince Charles. He is legally entitled to claim the throne once the Queen passes away. There is nothing that can alter this event.

Look again at the passage in Romans 8:17 *"we are heirs of God – and co-heirs with Christ"*. This means we are legally able to receive all that Jesus has because we are co-heirs with Christ. In other words whatever Christ has we have access to the very same. We do not have limited access, we have total and complete access, the same privileges and rights as Christ. Paul states in Ephesians:

"And God raised us up with Christ and seated us with Him in the Heavenly realms in Christ Jesus."

Ephesians 2:6

Just as Jesus is seated in the Heavenly realms, so too are we. Notice this is written in the past tense, therefore God has already done it. I have heard people suggest that this is a future event, but according to Paul we already **are** seated with Him. We are seated with Christ now. This is a privilege of being co-heirs. We get to partner with Jesus, we get to reign with Jesus; it is not something we have to wait for. We don't have to try and live up to a certain standard, we don't have to attain a certain level of maturity, there is no price we have to pay. This is part of the grace of God, it is freely given to us and it is impossible to earn. All we have to do is live as though we are seated with Him, live as though we are citizens of Heaven (Philippians 3:20) and so we live according to the culture of Heaven. We live our life from the culture of Heaven and not the earthly one, we allow His Spirit to dwell within us and replace the desires of this world with that of the Kingdom. We live with Heavenly values, we live as though we are heirs. If we could truly understand what it means to be co-heirs with Christ our lives would be different, my life is different. Part of being an heir is that we get to share in the authority of Christ.

I was spending time with Father recently and I felt He was talking to me about authority, my authority. Father said "When I give you an authority in a place, I give you an extra anointing too."

"All authority in Heaven and earth has been given to me...."

Matthew 28:18

Jesus has all the authority. If we do things in His name we carry that same authority. Just as a police officer has the authority of the law, the officer only has the authority when in uniform. If the police officer tries to stop you out of uniform you will likely drive on. When wearing the uniform you stop. The uniform distinguishes them as a police officer. If we go in the authority of God, we wear His anointing (His Spirit) which distinguishes us. We are carrying something of Him. What do we carry?

His presence is the anointing that is on us because of the authority in His Spirit. When we go and do exploits in His name we go in His authority and therefore we carry His presence. It is His presence that has the power to change the situation.

R Puttman puts it like this:

> *"Another aspect of the Holy Spirit in us is that with the Holy Spirit's presence comes spiritual authority."* [1]

The question is wherever we go and whatever we do, are we under His authority? Has He sent us? If so, I believe we should expect situations to change. I believe we should expect sickness to flee. Where His authority and therefore anointing is, there His presence is also. Therefore, there is nothing of the enemy that can stand against it.

The authority I speak about is a spiritual one. The Bible is clear:

> *"For our struggle is not against flesh and blood, but against the rulers, against the authorities, against the powers of this dark world and against the spiritual forces of evil in the Heavenly realms."*
>
> *Ephesians 6:12*

Wherever we go we go in His name, then the spiritual forces of evil have to submit to the power of Jesus within us. Jesus in the great commission said, *"All authority has been given to me ...."* (Matthew.28:18), also according to the gospel of Mark:

> *"Go into all the world and preach the good news to all creation. Whoever believes and is baptized will be saved, but whoever does not believe will be condemned. And these signs will accompany those who believe: In my name they will drive our demons; they will speak in new tongues; they will pick up snakes with their hands; and when they drink deadly poison, it will not hurt them at all; they will place their hands on sick people, and they will get well". After the Lord Jesus had spoken to them, He was*

---

[1] Puttman, R. (2013) *School of Kingdom Ministry Manual.* Coaching Saints Publications. p. 55.(Permission granted)

taken up into Heaven and He sat at the right hand of God. Then the disciples went out and preached everywhere, and the Lord worked with them and confirmed His word by the signs that accompanied it."

Mark 16:15-20

Jesus had just commissioned His disciples. He had anointed them and encouraged them that they would see signs and wonders. As we undertake the Great Commission, we should expect sickness to be healed and bodies to be restored and demons to flee. Notice the authority is not given to us, but if we go in His name, we then carry the authority which is in the name. We carry the mighty name of Jesus; we are carrying His presence into those places we are sent.

If we are carrying His presence wherever we go, we should expect to see healings and we should expect to see blind eyes open. We should expect to see the impossible become possible. Just as if a plain clothes police officer were to stop you in the street, there will be times when you might stop, but clearly if that same officer stops you whilst in uniform, then there is a greater chance that you will stop. Let us wear the 'uniform of Heaven', let us act in the authority of His name and in His presence.

Let's keep pressing in for an increase in the Kingdom of God to come. Let us keep pressing in for the impossible to become possible. Let us discover where He has called us, let us find out to whom He has called us, and I believe with that we will carry the 'uniform' the Holy Spirit. I believe this in turn will lead us to be moving in the authority of Father God, we then can and will see greater things.

As heirs and co-heirs with Christ we have been given the anointing. In other words, we are carrying the authority of the name of Jesus therefore we have everything we need. Let us move and minister in that anointing, let us believe who we are, let us understand where we sit and let us understand the power we have in the name of Jesus. There is no name greater in Heaven or on the earth than that of the name of Jesus. I heard Bill Johnson once say, "If Jesus has all the authority; therefore it is true to say that the enemy has none." The enemy is fighting a losing battle. With the anointing of Jesus, we are fighting a battle that Jesus has already won.

The passage we started with at the beginning of this chapter has much more to say about our identity.

We are adopted as His sons

Father has adopted us into His family. We now have the rights of our new family and we bear the name of our new family. Names in the Bible are significant; they tell you something of who the person is. For example, Moses means "to draw out". Pharaoh's daughter gave him this name after she had rescued him from the river Nile (Ex.2:10). He had literally been drawn out of the river Nile. Joseph means "May Jehovah give increase". Joseph rose to a great place within Egypt after he was sold into slavery. Finally, the name Abraham means "Father of many". In today's time names do not always have such significant meanings; however, names do have power within them. Take Prince William for example. Because of his name and title we know he is special, we know he has influence. So it is true of us. Because we have been adopted into His family we now bear His name, and so this gives us an authority.

I will expand further on the fruits of being adopted as a child of God in the next chapter.

We are children of God

The Bible contains a lot of passages about us being children of God. It is Father's heart that we truly know that we are His children.

"Yet to all who received Him, to those who believed in His name, have the right to become children of God – children born not of natural descent, nor of human decision or a husband's will, but born of God."

John 1:12

It is our right as believers to be called His children. When someone has a right they have a legitimate claim, a legal claim. We have a lawful entitlement; we can justifiably use the title child of God. Just as I can call my father 'Dad' and no one else can reasonably do that, so we can describe ourselves as children of God.

"You are all sons of God through faith in Christ Jesus, for all of you who were baptised into Christ have clothed yourselves with Christ."

Galatians 3:26

It is because of our faith in Jesus that we have this legal right to be called children of God. It is only because of Him that we are adopted into God's family and therefore are called His children. It is part of our identity; it is part of our inheritance that we have this title. It is not a title we were born with, but it is rightfully ours now. My wife can rightfully call herself a 'Russell' because of the legal agreement, our marriage. Before she had no right or claim to either my name or my belongings.

It is because of the marriage agreement all that has changed. In fact, with that same legal agreement she chooses to no longer use her maiden name, once she said her vows and signed the marriage certificate.

It is because of the covenant of the shed blood of Jesus that we now have the right to be called His children. We no longer have a right to be children of darkness, we have relinquished that name. We now are known by our new name and title. It is time that we lived as though that title is ours, as though we are children of God, because that is who we are in the here and now, this is not something we can hope for in the future.

"I will be a Father to you, and you will be my sons and daughters, says the Lord Almighty."

2 Corinthians 6:18

Not only do we have a right to be called children of God, but notice that God says He will be a Father to us. We are His children. We are His sons and daughters.

Another passage that talks about our right to be called children of God is found in Galatians:

"But when the time had fully come, God sent His Son, born of a woman, born under law, to redeem those under law, that we might receive the full rights as sons. Because you are sons, God sent the Spirit of His Son into our hearts, the Spirit who calls out, "Abba, Father." So you are no longer a slave, but a son; and since you are a son, God has made you an heir."

Galatians 4:4-7

These verses give us an understanding of what it means to be called His children; it tells us what happened as a result of the covenantal transaction of Jesus. Firstly, God sent His Spirit to live within us, but not just with us, but to live in us. We have become the home of the Spirit, or as Paul says our body is a temple of the Holy Spirit (1 Corinthians 6:19). We are the very place where God resides; He chooses to call us home.

Secondly we are no longer slaves. The suggestion here is that once we were slaves. However, Paul appears to draw a distinction, it appears that we cannot be both a slave and a son, we are either a slave or we are a son. The consequence of being a son means we have moved from slavery into sonship. Jack Frost, in his book 'Spiritual Slavery to Spiritual Sonship' suggests that without sonship we are orphans. He goes further and proposes that orphans are slaves.[2] It is possible to live spiritually as orphans, in other words to have an orphan spirit. One of the consequences of this is that we have closed our hearts from receiving love and living freely in that love, and consequently we find we struggle to give that love to others; we might feel alone and isolated. However, sonship is simply to have revelation in our hearts that we are His children. We can live in our identity as children of God and with that we feel accepted. As we shall see later there is a significant difference between being a slave and being a son. As Leif Hetland suggests "Orphans live for love, sons live from love."[3] As a result of us being called children of God we are no longer slaves and orphans, we are sons.

---

[2] Frost, J. (2006) *Spiritual Slavery to Spiritual Sonship*. Shippensburg: Destiny Image Publishers. p.120-129. He gives 20 characteristics of an orphan and highlights the difference in thinking like a son and an orphan.

[3] Hetland, L. (2013) *Baptism of Love*. Published by Leif Hetland. p.35. (Permission granted)

The word 'father' may have a negative connotation for you. You may not have had a good role model for a father and as such you may shy away from the idea of Father God being your father. In fact we will, very often without knowing it, project our understanding of fathers on to Father God, and it is only as we begin to forgive our earthly fathers and move forward into sonship that Father God can reveal His true heart for us.

It is important for us to realise that Father God is not like our earthly fathers. Even if our earthly father was great, Father God is even better.

Let's take a look at the story of the prodigal son.

"Jesus continued: "There was a man who had two sons. The younger one said to his father, 'Father, give me my share of the estate.' So he divided his property between them. Not long after that, the younger son got together all he had, set off for a distant country and there squandered his wealth in wild living. After he had spent everything, there was a severe famine in that whole country, and he began to be in need. So he went and hired himself out to a citizen of that country, who sent him to his fields to feed pigs. He longed to fill his stomach with the pods that the pigs were eating, but no one gave him anything. "When he came to his senses, he said, 'How many of my father's hired servants have food to spare, and here I am starving to death! **I will set out and go back to my father and say to him: Father, I have sinned against Heaven and against you. I am no longer worthy to be called your son; make me like one of your hired servants.'** *So he got up and went to his father. "But while he was still a long way off, his father saw him and was filled with compassion for him; he ran to his son, threw his arms around him and kissed him. "The son said to him, 'Father, I have sinned against Heaven and against you. I am no longer worthy to be called your son. "But the father said to his servants,* **'Quick! Bring the best**

robe and put it on him. Put a ring on his finger and sandals on his feet. Bring the fattened calf and kill it. Let's have a feast and celebrate. **For this son of mine was dead and is alive again;** he was lost and is found.' So they began to celebrate. "Meanwhile, the older son was in the field. When he came near the house, he heard music and dancing. So he called one of the servants and asked him what was going on. 'Your brother has come,' he replied, 'and your father has killed the fattened calf because he has him back safe and sound.'"

Luke 15:11-27 (emphasis added)

Firstly let's look at the younger son's thoughts. After he had squandered his inheritance he does not see himself worthy to be called a son; he was willing to become a servant. He felt shame, he thought his claim to be called a son was lost. He thought his only hope was to return to the family home as a servant. In his mind he had walked away from his role as a son and his father would only accept him back if he were to return as a servant. Servanthood in the family home, for the son, was better than where he found himself.

The response of the father, however, was not quite what the son was expecting. For the father it was about his son's return. Notice the father welcomed him back with open arms. The father was ready to welcome the son home, not as a slave, but as a son in the same position as he was before he left. Each of the items placed upon the son upon his return signify the love the Father has for his son. Let's look at each item individually.

Robe

The robe signified his position as a son was being restored. It speaks of forgiveness; the younger son was completely accepted back to the family. It not only demonstrated this fact to the son, but to all those who saw him wear it. It confirmed that the father had love and mercy for his son; he was showing complete acceptance for him. The son returns covered in shame, guilt, and sin, but the father accepts him as he is. His shame is covered by a new robe, a robe of sonship. In fact the robe more than covers his shame, it completely removed it, shame is no longer his portion. It is no longer who he is and shame is no longer his identity. He is able to move from shame to sonship.

Ring

The ring was a symbol of affection and authority. It was a sign of wealth and dignity. The ring was used when a decree or ruling had been agreed in government. We read in the book of Esther:

"Now write another decree in the King's name on behalf of the Jews as seems best to you, and seal it with the king's signet ring – for no document written in the King's name and sealed with his ring can be revoked"

Esther 8:8

Genesis 41:42 tells us that Pharaoh gave Joseph his ring when he was installed into office; Joseph now had authority. The son would have understood the significance of this ring and although he felt he didn't deserve affection he would soon have realised that servanthood was not who he was. With the ring being placed on his finger he knew that he was being given authority, something a servant would not have. He had the authority of the father; he was able to wear the authority as a son, as a member of the family.

Sandals

The son returned home without shoes. Culturally this was a symbol of his poverty and the fact that he had lost everything. Servants and slaves were the ones who walked around barefoot. Yet for the father, the son had not lost everything, he was not destitute. The sign of being in poverty was replaced with a sign of riches, of love and of affection. As the father gave his younger son shoes, it was a sign that said you are my son, I give you all that I have, as a son you have access to my riches, and therefore you are not in poverty anymore. It was the final sign to both the son and those who saw him that his position of sonship was once again restored, along with all the blessings that came with that.

The three items placed upon the son are items that would have demonstrated to all who witnessed it that the son was restored into his father's household. Although the prodigal son left the family home and squandered all he was given, there was still room for him in his father's household. There was still a place for him at his father's table.

The son returned with nothing and expected nothing, but his father gave him everything. He was given a robe demonstrating the complete forgiveness and total approval the father had for the son, it was a robe of love and protection. He was given the ring, which demonstrated all the riches of the father were now part of the son, he now had complete access his father's wealth. Finally, he was given sandals demonstrating the son's return to sonship, with all the blessings included with that. You and I as co- heirs with Christ have the same. We have been given a robe of love and protection. A robe that signifies that the guilt and shame we once carried are no longer ours to carry, it has been replaced with a robe of righteousness. We have a ring, the ring of authority and the full riches of Christ, and we also have received the sandals of sonship. We came with nothing but have been given everything.

For the father the son's return was never about his position, it had always been about his presence with the father. The son had always been a member of the family, and as such the father wanted his son back in his presence, back in his care as a member of the family. All the Father wants of us is to be in His presence, to be in a place of rest as a member of His family.

In the eyes of the father, there was never any thought that the son would return as anything less than who he was when he went away. He left as a son and so he returned as a son. There is nothing that can change the status of him being a son. He was the father's son and that would always remain.

Our Heavenly Father always wants the best for His children. There is nothing that can change our position of sonship if we continue to put our faith in Jesus. Just like the prodigal son in the story we are clothed in a robe, the robe of approval, we have a ring, the ring of authority upon our finger and we also wear sandals, the sandals of riches; all of which are in Christ Jesus.

It is Father's will that we live this life of sonship, that we know deep in our hearts that He has a love for us before we do anything, and that we always have access to Him.

Father God loves us not for what we do or how good we are. Father loves us and calls us His children, His sons and daughters, simply by believing in Him. He loves us, we are His children just by being who we are.

The Spirit Himself testifies to our sonship

Holy Spirit witnesses and confirms the truth that we are children of God. In a court of law a witness is brought in to confirm or strengthen the case. They will testify that what is being said is true. Holy Spirit is confirming with us, with our spirit, that what is being said is true. We have the Spirit of God living in our hearts; it is this Holy Spirit that confirms to our spirits that we are His children. It is time to listen to Him, He is telling us the truth, He is bearing witness, He is confirming what we read, that we have become sons of the Father.[4]

We inherit all that Father has for us

An inheritance comes when there is a death; Jesus had to die in order that we receive this inheritance. The very same inheritance that Jesus Himself received. The inheritance is for now; we have access to it today. As we have just read in Luke 15:11-32 in the story of the Lost Son, so often churches talk and preach about the son who went away and wasted the inheritance he was to receive. Let's look at this culturally. In the culture of the time it was considered disrespectful to ask for your inheritance early. But notice there is no hint that the father is angry or upset at the younger son's request. Now let's look closely at the older son who is often not mentioned as frequently in our churches.

> *"The older brother became angry and refused to go in. So his father went out and pleaded with him. But he answered his father, 'Look! All these years I've been slaving for you and never disobeyed your orders. Yet you never gave me even a young goat so I could celebrate with my friends. But*

---

[4] Culturally sons are the people who inherit; they are seen as having authority, therefore when the Bible talks about being a son, it is simply saying that all believers have authority and receive an inheritance.

when this son of yours who has squandered your property with prostitutes comes home, you kill the fattened calf for him!' "My son,' the father said, 'you are always with me, and everything I have is yours.'"

Luke 15:28-31

The older son had always been with the father, he had always obeyed the orders of his father. However, he had failed in one simple thing, he had not understood that he always had access to his father's inheritance. Notice his father's response "everything I have is yours". Is it possible that our Heavenly Father is saying the same to us? Is it possible that we are missing out today because we simply have not understood, we have not grasped that what is His is by inheritance ours also. It is available to us today. How different could our lives be if we understood and really believed this, if we allowed ourselves to take hold of what is rightfully ours today?

We have access to the Father

I remember a picture Father gave me not so long back of a clock that had no hands on it. Father was saying He is not restrained by time; He is always present and always wanting to spend time with me. There is never a time when He will reject me or ask me to come back later. We have complete access to Him; He is always waiting, looking, listening for when I come to Him.

Father always has an open door to us. Father is never too busy. Figuratively speaking it is like the Father will always put down whatever He is doing to spend time with each one of us. We all have access to the Father. You may not have had a father that always had time for you; maybe he was always at work or at this meeting or that engagement. I would encourage you to forgive your father and ask Father God if you believe a lie about Him, then ask Him what the truth is. So often, as I have had the privilege of leading people through Sozo ministry, I see that people's understanding of Father God is shaped by their experience of their earthly father. However, I have seen countless people come to experience the Father's true love by this simple process of forgiveness and replacing lies with truth. I have seen Father lovingly and gently restore the intended connection between Himself and that person. He shows them what He thinks of them, He tells them how He sees them. It is a beautiful moment when the person receives this truth and revelation, without fail each person who has received these truths from Father has commented how they feel different, they feel lighter and have a renewed sense of peace. After one session my wife and I received this testimony of how this person was impacted and how they experienced the love of the Father:

> *"I am a 24 year old young lady who was orphaned at the age of 7; molested by my father at the age of 5 and watched him beat up my mother all the time as we shared the same room. I was angry at God for a very long time and did not understand why he allowed these things to happen. So I became self-destructive and just went on living life so something would kill me. I have had two abortions in my life and have tried to kill myself several times. I had the lowest self-esteem and zero self-love. I was a living wreck.*
>
> *I have never in my 24 years of living experienced God the way I did at the Sozo. It was so real God showed me who I was and erased all the lies I had been believing about myself.*

Through the Sozo God was able to open my eyes and just gave me a new sense of being. I am not the same young lady who walked into their house. I came out renewed.

I am a new creation. I am looking forward to my next Sozo and just growing in Christ and seeking Him every day.

Depression, anxiety and everything dark is not my portion any more. God gave me a new heart. God showed me visions at the Sozo, the most beautiful thing of all He showed me just what he thought of me by showing me a vision of Him proposing to me. He loves me. I believe that more than anything. God showed up and I am a new creation."

Father wants to reveal His true nature to His children. It is the delight of the Father to reveal His goodness, to reveal His love for each one of His children. I believe a common misconception we have is that God needs us to fulfil His will. Father is more than able to do what He wants when He wants to. We are all more than capable of being able to serve Him, people have been serving Him since the creation. Our service to Him has never been broken, however, our relationship was broken. Jesus came to restore that broken relationship, the relationship that the Father intended for us to enjoy in the first place. It is His nature to reveal His immense, intimate, and passionate love to each of us, to reveal who He is. When we come to receive the revelation more fully of who He is, then we can begin to understand who we are. I believe once we begin to understand who we are then our heart will begin to change and we will begin to live in our true identity. It is time to understand who we are and whose we are. When we know whose we are then we can truly be who we are. It is out of who we belong to that we can truly be who we are supposed to be.

Malawian culture is to serve not out of a relationship, but out of a duty. Whilst living there my wife and I have had the privilege of mentoring a young Malawian church leader. During this time he began to realise who Father is and subsequently who his identity is in. He experienced the revelation that what we do for Father comes out of our relationship with Him. He felt such a sense of freedom, understanding, and a revelation of the truth of who his Father is; a good and loving Father.

Prayer:

Father thank You that we are co- heirs with Christ and that is who I am. Father thank you that You want us to be in relationship with You and You want us to understand Your love for us, the love You have is far greater than any other. I open my heart to You for You to reveal that love You have for me so that I may begin to move from orphan thinking to thinking as a son. I thank You I can call You Father, that I have complete unrestricted access to You and You always want to spend time we me. Father I ask that you would reveal to me areas where my earthly father has restricted my view of You and reveal to me Your true nature.

Mark Russell

Adopted as Sons

"For He chose us in Him before the creation of the world to be holy and blameless in His sight. In love He predestined us for adoption to sonship through Jesus Christ, in accordance with His pleasure and will."

Ephesians 1:4-5

Adoption was not an idea after God realised everything was not going according to plan. Adoption in Christ is the way God chose to create His family even before He created the world. Adoption was His plan.

"While we were still sinners Christ died for us."

Romans 5:8

We were in a state of uncleanliness, and in the natural God would not have adopted us because He is holy and we were not. The moment we recognise what He did on the cross for us and we accept Him, we become clean and so Father by His grace adopts us into His family. The adopted son, you and I, are received into our new family and we can assume all of the rights and responsibilities associated with it.

The word adoption in the New Testament is translated from the Greek word *huiothesia* which means 'the placing of an adult son' and refers to the formal act of recognising the maturity of an adult son.[1] The concept of adoption into sonship in Roman culture is a legal term referring to the full legal standing of an adopted male heir. In fact, according to Roman law it goes further; an adopted child was firstly chosen (we will look more into this in the chapter on being chosen), in other words desired. But maybe just as powerful was that this adoption was permanent, the new parents had no rights to disown their adopted child. As a result this child received a new identity, all ties are completely cut from their former family. The adopted child had new rights and will have new responsibilities. The adopted child became an heir; they had a legal right to any inheritance of the new family. For us as believers this means that we are fully loved, we are fully desired, we have a new identity through Jesus and we are created for Heaven, and with immediate effect we are heirs of God.

We are *now* adopted into the family of God; everything that had to be done has been accomplished. Once we accept Jesus as our saviour we become part the Heavenly family. This is not something that happens in the future, when we meet Father in Heaven, but is a reality right now here on earth. This is a true fact whether we believe it or not. This will have a huge impact on our lives and how we live if we can start to believe it; that we are sons of the living God and He is our Father.

---

[1] Nelson Study Bible, (1997) NKJV. Nashville: Thomas Nelson Publishers.

Let us look at other New Testament passages:

"For you did not receive a spirit that makes you a slave again to fear, but you received the spirit of sonship. And by Him we cry. "Abba, Father""

Romans 8:15

The Spirit you received does not make you a slave so that you live in fear again; rather the Spirit you received brought about your adoption to sonship. And it is by Him that we cry *"Abba, Father."*

Notice that it is the Holy Spirit who brings about our adoption. The Holy Spirit is the Spirit of Jesus. Therefore, because of the death and resurrection of Jesus we have received adoption into His family. The Holy Spirit takes us from being slaves to being adopted as sons. Slaves operate out of fear. Slaves operate out of a need to earn favour. Sons, however, operate out of freedom and out of a secure identity. They know their position is secure; they don't need to work to receive the status of sons. We have been removed from slavery; we have been removed from fear. Fear is not part of our new family life; they were of the old family, the family we used to belong to. We are now adopted into sonship (Romans 8:15) with the Father, we have become sons of God and Jesus has become our brother (Hebrews 2:11) and therefore there is no need to fear. With Almighty God as our Father what is there to fear? Who is there that is more powerful than He? If we live from the place of truly understanding this revelation of our position as adopted sons, and we know who we are, we can have the confidence to not fear.

Paul in his letter to the Romans says:

"What then, shall we say in response to this? If God is for us, who can be against us? He did not spare His own Son, but gave Him up for us all – how will He not also, along with Him, graciously give us all things?"

Romans 8:31-32

Father God gave up His only Son in order for us to be adopted into His family. God sent His son Jesus as a man so that mankind can become sons and daughters of God. It follows then that now we have no need to fear, there is nothing that can come against us because we have the adoptive rights as His sons. Just as an earthly father should protect and look out for his child, how much more is this true about our Heavenly Father. He is perfect (Matthew 5:48) and so He will protect and look out for His children. God really is for us.

Have you heard a child say *"Do you know who my Dad is?"* We can truly say this. Our Father is God Almighty, He is the one that created the world. He is the one who gave us life. He is the one who made all things and He is the one who is all powerful. It really is not a fair fight; in fact the fight against our enemy it is not a fight at all. We come under the love and protection of our Abba Father and as a result nothing can come against us, we have all we need to overcome. We come to Him; we hide in His presence and allow His peace to fill our hearts. Father speaks and that is the end of it. He is our Father who will always come to our aid and protect us.

Trials

Our adoption has happened; we have the Holy Spirit living inside us. As Paul writes

In His Image

"Not only so, but we ourselves, who have the first fruits of the Spirit, groan inwardly as we wait eagerly for our adoption to sonship, the redemption of our bodies."

Romans 8:23

The phrase 'first fruits' could refer to a foretaste[2] of that which is to come. The Holy Spirit is a guarantee of what is to come (which we will look at later). Our adoption has happened, but this by no means suggests however from now on our life is easy, it does not mean we don't go through trials anymore. Trials are part of life, we should never expect to be free from them, but we know that these trials develop and mature us:

"In all this you greatly rejoice, though now for a little while you may have had to suffer grief in all kinds of trials. These have come so that the proven genuineness of your faith – of greater worth than gold, which perishes even though refined by fire – may result in praise, glory and honour when Jesus Christ is revealed. Though you have not seen Him, you love Him; and even though you do not see Him now, you believe in Him and are filled with an inexpressible and glorious joy, for you are receiving the end result of your faith, the salvation of your souls."

1 Peter 1:6-9

Peter suggests trials are part of life, but as our faith is proven as genuine through trials, we can then give Jesus all of the glory, honour and praise.

James says:

"Consider it pure joy, my brothers, whenever you face trials of many kinds, because you know that the testing of your faith develops perseverance.

---

[2] The New Living Translation translates the Greek word *aparche* as foretaste

Perseverance must finish its work so that you may be mature and complete, not lacking anything."

James 1:2-4

James is encouraging us to rejoice in these trials as they are opportunities for us to grow and learn. We are encouraged to rejoice during these times because joy and thankfulness is the correct response. To go through such difficulties in any other way can lead to resentment. As we face these trials with faith in Him, then we are able to keep going. It is not the trials themselves that develop perseverance, but rather our attitude of faith during those seasons. As we go through these trials, we are able to remember how God has worked before and therefore we can be encouraged the next time. We could trust God then, therefore we can trust Him now. We go from strength to strength.

Or as Paul puts it as we go through these trials, we are able to move from being a child to being a mature son. Romans 8 says:

"*For as many who are led by the Spirit of God they are sons of God*"

Romans 8:14 (KJV)

The Greek word here used for sons, means mature sons. Therefore, there is a process that takes place which sometimes involve trials, as we grow from being immature children to being mature sons. The Holy Spirit living in us is the beginning of that process. We have the promise of sonship, we are adopted now. But we will one day, when we are taken to be with Him in Heaven, be free from these trials.

Our Guarantee

Paul encourages us with the same thought in Ephesians:

"And you also were included in Christ when you heard the word of truth, the gospel of your salvation. Having believed, you were marked in Him with a seal, the promised Holy Spirit, who is a deposit guaranteeing our inheritance until the redemption of those who are God's possession – to the praise of His glory."

Ephesians 1:13-14

The Holy Spirit has marked us, we have been sealed as belonging to the Father. Many years ago when I was a child I wrote a letter to the Queen. When I received a response, even before I opened the envelope, I knew where it had come from. On the back of the envelope was a seal; it was the Queen's seal. The seal told me the letter was important, it told me who the letter was from. The seal we are marked with is the seal of the Holy Spirit; it is because of Him that we are guaranteed the inheritance from the Father. The Holy Spirit is also a deposit, just as an engagement ring is like a deposit of the promise of marriage. He is a deposit of the promise of eternal life, but also by the Holy Spirit we are adopted.

Our adoption is guaranteed by the fact that the Holy Spirit is living inside of us. It is not something that we can hope for in vain or maybe something that sounds like a nice thing to have. As believers we have this, it is a right, it is something that can and should be enjoyed now.

"But when the set time had fully come, God sent His Son, born of a woman, born under the law to redeem those under the law, that we might

receive adoption to sonship. Because you are His sons, God sent the Spirit of His Son into our hearts, the Spirit who calls out, "Abba, Father."'

Galatians 4:4-6

Adoption is complete

Before Christ came into the world mankind was under the law, a law that was impossible to fully follow and adhere to. As a result we were born under that same law. However, Christ came that we would, through acceptance of Him, be able to move from slavery to the law to being sons adopted into His family. Jesus modelled how we are to live as mature sons adopted into His family. He showed us that it is possible to live a life of grace and not live as slaves under the law. Adoption brings about a complete change. As adopted sons we no longer live under the old way of life, we no longer have to live like slaves; we can live as free children. Everything in our life before we accepted Jesus has been forgotten, it has been forgiven and all our debts have been wiped clean. As we continue to ask for forgiveness, He continues to freely forgive us and we can be certain that the slate will remain clean. According to Roman law when the adoption was complete, there was nothing left to be done. That child had all the rights that any naturally born child of the family had. The adopted child lost all rights and claim on the old family. The child was legally and rightfully a new person, so much so that any debts of his natural parents were no longer their responsibility. It was as if the child never had any connection with his previous family. We now have a new family, we are no longer part of the kingdom of darkness, we are part of the kingdom of light, the family of God, and the debts we owed were paid by Jesus on our behalf.

The adoption we have received is a complete one; it is by this adoption that we are free of our old way of life. We can now live our life as new people, new creations:

> *"Therefore if anyone is in Christ, he is a new creation; the old has gone, the new has come."*
>
> *2 Corinthians 5:17*

Due to our adoption, not only is our old way of life no longer part of who we are, but the truth is that we are different, the old has truly gone. Our old nature, our pride, our love of ourselves, our sin, everything that made up our life before, is now gone, it is dead; it is nailed to the cross. Therefore we no longer have to live that old way of life. It is a continual process as we continue to renew our mind (Romans 12:2) and think the same way about us that the Father does. We are now a new creation. This is not something we have done by our own efforts. We have not just decided that we shall no longer live like the old man; the truth is we cannot just decide to change our ways. We are new creations, God has re-created us. He did not simply wipe away the old you, He literally created something different and we now have a new DNA, the DNA we now have is His. We are a new creation. And so it is now possible for us to live this new life.

With Father we have a new position, new privileges, a new family and a new name. Iain Emberson provides a fuller picture:

> *"The spiritual use of the word 'adoption' signifies the placing of a newborn child, in the spiritual sense, into the position of privilege and responsibility attached to an adult son. The question arises as to why a naturally born child needs to be*

> *adopted. Are we not, after all, 'born again'? It is here that the true meaning of "adoption" comes in; because in the New Testament, "adoption" refers to a positional advance. The new believer is advanced positionally to his majority, even though at the time of salvation he is spiritually immature, a "babe in Christ".*
>
> *Because spiritual adoption takes place at the moment of salvation, there is really no period of childhood experience recognised for believers. The Christian has been placed into the privilege, liberty, and duty of a full-grown adult. Spiritual adoption imposes the same way of life on all children of God. This requirement is reasonable because the Christian life is to be lived in the sustaining and upholding power of the Holy Spirit. And this provision is available as much for one person as for another."* [3]

Paul recognised that adoption symbolised God's love and grace and therefore by right we are a member of His family. We are not on the outside looking in, but rather we are on the inside looking out. In other words, we the believer have all rights of inheritance of an eternal life with God.

Some believers have been under, I believe, the false impression that our adoption is something that we can hope for in the future or perhaps something that we can attain or earn. I believe that our adoption is something we have now, something that we should be living today, we are adopted into His family. This adoption is now; it is for all believers and not just the elect few or those who live a good life. The phrase 'I'm not spiritual

---

[3] Emberson, I. (2016) *Christianity in View*. Available at: http://christianityinview.com/biblestudies/adoption.html (Accessed: 28th March 2020) (Permission granted)

enough' should no longer be part of our vocabulary, it has nothing to do with us but has everything to do with Jesus. I quoted 2 Corinthians 5:17 earlier but if we read on to verse 18 Paul says "All this from God, who reconciled us to Himself through Christ". You see the Father found the son, the son did not find the Father.

We have been adopted. We are, through Jesus, a legal male heir with all the rights of any child. We have lost all ties to our old way of life, our previous family. We are now part of the Kingdom of Light and not the Kingdom of darkness. The Kingdom of darkness no longer has any legal control, we are truly free from any claim or influence it may try to hold over us. We are now part of the Kingdom of light.

We are a new creation because of what Christ accomplished on the cross. Therefore, we are adopted into sonship with the Father because of the cross. Can we earn our salvation? No. In the same way we cannot earn our inheritance as adopted children of God. We receive it all by His grace. I recall hearing someone once say "Grace is receiving what we don't deserve; mercy is not receiving what we do deserve." In other words mercy withholds the consequence we deserved, whereas grace provides us with unmerited favour.

We need to understand that by His grace we have been given everything that we don't deserve. We do not deserve adoption, but it is true to say that because of His mercy we do not receive that which we do deserve. Because we have been adopted by His grace we now receive all the blessings that come with that including mercy. If we have received grace, then we have by default received mercy.

Grace and mercy go together. It is impossible to have one without the other. They go hand in hand, and it is because of both of these, mercy and grace, that we get to be called adopted sons. We are no longer aliens but fellow citizens and members of God's household (Ephesians 2:19). We are not just forgiven, we are adopted as sons and consequently all of our old way of life has been wiped away. We now have complete access to the Father and all that Jesus has we also have.

Prayer:

Father I thank You that I have been adopted into Your family, that I am desired by You and that I am truly loved. Thank You that my old life is no more and because of the cross I have become a new creation. I thank you that what is Yours is legally mine; I have a legal right to all that You have. Thank You that because of my adoption into Your family not only can I call You Dad, but I have an identity as a child of God.

Intimacy

From the beginning of creation Father God desired to have an intimate relationship with us. His intention and original plan was for us to have the ability to be intimate with Him. He created us to be in a relationship, an intimate relationship with Him.

So what does it mean to be intimate? To be intimate with someone is to have a comprehensive or complete understanding or knowledge of someone. God wants to have a comprehensive knowledge of us, but more importantly He wants the same for us. For us to have such a knowledge, such an encounter with Him, that it transforms our thinking and our experience of Him. Look at what Paul writes to the Colossians:

"I have become its servant by the commission God gave me to present to you the word of God in all its fullness – the mystery that has been hidden for ages and generations, but is now disclosed to the saints. To them God

has chosen to make known among the Gentiles the glorious riches of this mystery, which is Christ in you, the hope of glory."

Colossians 1:25-27

If something is not known it could be said it is a mystery. But note Paul says that God has disclosed or made known this mystery, but to whom is this mystery made known to? To the saints which is you and I, those who believe the good news of the gospel of Jesus Christ. So what is the mystery that is made known? It is simply Christ in us.

We read in John's Gospel that Jesus says:

"I have made You known to them, and will continue to make You known in order that the love You have for me may be in them and that I myself may be in them."

John 17:26

The Father sent Jesus, that we might know the Father, that we might experience the love of the Father, that we might be intimate with Him and He with us. This is why Jesus says "I have made You known to them". Intimacy works both ways. For example, within a married couple it is difficult for one partner to be intimate without the other reciprocating that intimacy. Jesus revealed the Father, He made Him known to us, because He wanted us to be intimate with Father and intimacy comes from a place of knowing.

We have seen in the chapter 'Made in His Image' that not only were we created in the image of God, but also in Genesis we read that when man was created we were deemed to be very good (Genesis 1:31). All other aspects of the creation were good, but mankind was very good. We are described as very good because we are created in His image and we have the capability to experience intimacy with Father God. It is only mankind who is able to experience this with the Father, and so His purpose of revealing who He is, is now complete. It is with mankind that He is able to share His nature and His character with. He is an intimate Father and we are designed to be intimate with Him. We have the capacity within us to experience intimacy with the creator God, our Father in Heaven.

Through the creation of man Father saw His creation to be complete. This is because the Father can now reveal Himself. He can now demonstrate His love and be in an intimate relationship with His creation.

However, we all know the story; something happened that broke our intimacy with Him:

"So the Lord God banished him from the Garden of Eden to work the ground from which he had been taken. After He drove the man out, He placed on the East side of the Garden of Eden cherubim and a flaming sword flashing back and forth to guard the way to the tree of life."

Genesis 3:23-24

Man ate from the tree of good and evil and disobeyed God in this act. I believe obedience is a sign of intimacy with Father, and because of our disobedience our intimacy was broken. Consequently, Adam and Eve were banished from the Garden and therefore banished from being in the same place as the Father. A barrier was erected due to the Fall. Intimacy is difficult if two people are not in the same place, if there is a barrier between them. Because of the barrier of disobedience and sin, intimacy had been lost; there was a separation between God and His creation.

However, being banished from the Garden was not a punishment driven by anger, but a consequence of Adam and Eve's choice to eat from the Tree. Father God removed them from the Garden of Eden out of His care for them as His children for their protection. Father wanted to remove them from the Garden so they wouldn't remain eternally in their fallen nature. Therefore we see this act of mankind being removed from the garden was an act of a loving Father wanting to restore intimacy with mankind.

God created us in order that He might enjoy an intimate relationship with us. Even though mankind has disobeyed the Father He still had the desire to be intimate with us. His feelings for us have not changed, He does not have a Plan B. We were His one and only plan. There was never a question in the mind of God that He would give up on pursuing intimacy with mankind. He knew before He created us that the Fall would take place. Isaiah says:

"I make known the end from the beginning, from ancient times what is still to come. I say: My purpose will stand, and I will do what I please."

Isaiah 46:10

Although the Father knew from the beginning how things would turn out, His purposes never fail, He had already set things in motion to restore that intimacy; Jesus! Jesus was His way of demonstrating to mankind what intimacy looks like. Before Jesus came to earth intimacy with God was something that only a few could have, only a few were close to Him.

However, all of mankind were created for this intimacy with Him, not just a few.

As we saw earlier to be intimate is to know and be close to a person. Let's look at the life of Moses as I believe we can learn something of what intimacy with the Father looks like for you and I.

We read in the book of Psalms that God made His ways known to Moses (Psalm 103:7). This intimacy started when God reveals His name to Moses.

> *"Moses said to God, "Suppose I go to the Israelites and say to them, 'The God of your fathers has sent me to you,' and they ask me 'What is His name?' Then what shall I tell them?" God said to Moses, "I AM WHO I AM. This is what you are to say to the Israelites: 'I AM has sent me to you.'"*
>
> *Exodus 3:13-14*

This is the first instance of God revealing His name to man. Part of knowing someone is to know their name. Moses wanted to know the name of God, he wanted to understand who God was. As we saw earlier there is power in a name and as such the name tells someone a lot about who they are. Moses and God had an intimate relationship. More than just knowing His name, Moses wanted to know the ways of God.

> *"Moses said to the LORD, "You have been telling me, 'Lead these people,' but you have not let me know whom you will send with me. You have said, 'I know you by name and you have found favour with me.' If You are pleased with me, teach me Your ways so* **I may know You**

and continue to find favour with You. Remember that this nation is your people."

Exodus 33:12-13 (emphasis added)

God told Moses His name but Moses was not satisfied to leave it there, he wanted to go deeper. Moses wanted to know God, the ways of God, the nature of God, he wanted to know who God really was. Do we have such a longing, do we have such a desire? We have seen that God has made known His ways to us; He has made Himself available to be known. Just as Moses wanted to know more of God, just as he wanted a deeper relationship with Him, just as he wanted intimacy with Him, so it should be the same with each one of us. As we continue to read through the account of Moses we see that Moses did not stop there. He was not content with just knowing the name of God or the ways of God, he wanted to see His glory.

"The Moses said, "Now show me Your glory.""

Exodus 33:18

God's response however is an interesting one:

"But," he said, "you cannot see my face, for no one may see me and live.""

Exodus 33:20

It appears there is a correlation with the glory of God and the face of God. What greater intimacy is there between two people than to look at each other face to face, to lock eyes with each other and to look at each other with such depth? I think we can see here that Moses wanted to look at the Father face to face. He wanted to look deep into the eyes of his Creator. Every wedding I have been to, including my own, when the bride walks up the aisle or when the bride and groom are exchanging their vows, they look into each other's eyes; it is like they are revealing their souls to one another.

Because of Jesus, "no one may see me and live" changes and we can now freely come face to face with Father. As we gaze into His eyes we will be forever changed, our hearts will be transformed. We will see and experience His love for us in such a way that we will not just want to reflect that love back to Him, but to those around us too.

The more intimate we are the more intimacy we want. The more we know, the more we want to know. The deeper we are the deeper we want to go. Moses started by knowing the name of God, but soon that was not enough, He wanted to know Him and again even that was not sufficient. Moses wanted to see God face to face, that is why he said "now show me Your glory", he wanted to look into His eyes. The more Moses knew of God, the more he wanted to know. The more intimate Moses was with God, the deeper the intimacy Moses wanted. God was only too willing to meet Moses' requests because that is exactly what He wants of His children. It is as though Moses was the first to sing the Psalm David wrote:

"One thing I ask of the Lord, this is what I seek: that I may dwell in the house of the Lord all the days of my life, to gaze upon the beauty of the Lord and to seek Him in His temple."

Psalm 27:4

David, just like Moses, wanted to gaze upon God's beauty. In essence he wanted to see Him face to face, he wanted to be intimate with Him; he wanted to know more of Him.

Intimacy is a process, it doesn't just happen, it grows over time. Moses relationship with God started at the beginning, but soon His desire for intimacy grew from there. The intimacy Father wants each of us to experience is one of growth as we gain deeper revelation of His nature. Just as in any human relationship, there is a process. Normally we start by being introduced and from there we get to know each other. As we spend more time with each other we begin to know the heart of the person. We become friends with them; we begin to share deeper things with each other as we trust each other. Father is looking and longing for the same with you and with me. He wants to build a deep lasting intimate relationship with us.

In the book of Jeremiah we read:

*"But let him who boast, boast about this: that he understands and **knows** me..."*

Jeremiah 9:24 (emphasis added)

The word 'knows' here is the same as that when Moses describes knowing God. Jeremiah is saying that we can understand, we can know and experience God and His nature. The thought here is that we have seen what He is like, we have observed His loving ways and in the very same way we can experience everything we have observed, the knowing here is an experiential knowing. It is to know in our hearts. It's not just a factual piece of head knowledge but a deeper, intimate knowledge of who He is. We are being invited to taste and see that the Lord is good (Psalm 34:8). We are being encouraged to experience the goodness of the Lord. We are being called to understand who He is. First we experience and after we have experienced then we can truly understand Him, and by doing so we know Him in a deeper way. My wife knows I love her because she has first experienced my love. Experience leads to an understanding. We must first experience intimacy with Him then we can understand and know more of who He is.

The ultimate act of intimacy was displayed by Jesus, through His sacrifice on the cross.

> *"Greater love has no one than this, that he lay down his life for his friends. You are my friends if you do what I command. I no longer call you servants, because a servant does not know his master's business. Instead I have called you friends, for everything that I learned from my father I have made known to you."*
>
> *John 15:13-15*

Jesus laid down His life that we could know Him. We become His friends. Jesus draws a distinction between servants and friends. Servants do not have the option to be intimate with their masters. Servants have a factual head knowledge of their master. They know the name and what the master requires, but the knowledge is limited. Friends however, have the opportunity to know and experience first-hand all that the Father is. We can know and experience His goodness and His great love for us. Jesus says servants do not know the business of master, but friends know the will of the Father.

Because of the sacrifice of Jesus everything has been accomplished. The veil has been torn in two (Matthew 27:51). There is no longer division between us; intimacy with the Father is restored. In Old Testament times this was very difficult and certainly limited to a few. Now, however, everything has changed. It is because of Jesus that we can all experience true intimacy with God. Everything that Father is,

Jesus has made known to us. We no longer have to see God as a master; we can know Him as a friend. We can share secrets with each other, something slaves are unable to do, we can spend time with each other, and we can laugh and have fun together.

I remember a picture Father once shared with me of the two of us walking on a beach. In the picture suddenly He stops and He begins to splash me until eventually He was pushing me into the water in a fun and playful manner. Through this He was simply showing me that our relationship is one of friendship, love and intimacy. We are able to move from slaves of a master to friends of the Father. He wants that kind of relationship with each one of us, He wants us to not just be friends, but His children.

One of the biggest differences between servants and sons is that servants come from a mentality of earning. The relationship is about working for and earning money from the master; they work for their master's approval. Sons, however, live from a place of love, or as Leif Hetland put it:

> *"Servants work for a paycheck, Sons receive inheritance"* [1]

Servants only know what their master tells them. They don't have an understanding of the mind of the master and know nothing of the personal life of their master. A servant is task oriented, they are driven by doing the right thing for their master. Their goal is to obey, often to the letter, exactly what the master requires of them. If they stray from that then they

---

[1] Hetland, L. (2013) *Baptism of Love*. Published by Leif Hetland. p.28. (Permission granted)

are likely not to remain with the master. Their very success depends on their obedience.

Friends, however, have a different focus, they have an advantage over a servant. Friends are not so much concerned about obedience. Whilst there should always be a place for obedience, a friend knows the more intimate details, and so a friend is more concerned with the heart of the matter. If a friend asks me to do something for them, I am free to evaluate what has been asked, I am free to question and maybe discuss a better way. I know that we will remain friends no matter what my response might be, I am free to express my thoughts and opinions as the relationship is not based on fear but the friendship is based on freedom. A servant often lives from a place of fear; friends live from a place of freedom. Too often many believers still have that servant mentality. They are not living from a place of freedom and intimacy; they are not living as a son. We as believers are able to serve Him out of a place of intimacy, we serve out of sonship.

Paul understood the link between sacrifice and intimacy. Let us look at the following passage:

"But whatever was to my profit I now consider loss for the sake of Christ. What is more, I consider everything a loss compared to the surpassing greatness of knowing Christ Jesus My Lord, for whose sake I have lost all things."

Philippians 3:7-8

Paul was willing to sacrifice everything to the point of death, yet his main desire was to know Christ. Paul is saying that a personal or intimate relationship with Jesus should be the heart's desire of each of our lives. He is willing to sacrifice all he has in order to know Christ more. He will do anything in order to have a deeper, more intimate experiential knowledge of Him.

I believe that to be intimate with Father there are some simple steps we can take that will allow us to go deeper with Him. The list of steps are not exhaustive, but steps we have explored throughout this chapter.

Desire

The first step to intimacy is to have desire. As we read Psalm 27:4 earlier *"One thing I ask of the Lord, this is what I seek:"* David has one thing that he seeks. He has a sole focus; he has a deep desire for God, and God alone. He knows that only God will satisfy, he has that intimate understanding of God.

Also in Psalm 63 we read:

"O God, You are my God, earnestly I seek You; my soul thirsts for You, my body longs for You, in a dry and weary land where there is no water."

Psalm 63:1

There is nothing else that is more satisfying than to know God. He and only He will suffice; only He is the answer and consequently David has an intense longing to be with God.

Let's look at three stories (paraphrased in my own words) from the time of Jesus. In each of the stories we will see that despite everything the characters were going through there was a part of them that knew God. They had knowledge that said God is the water for my soul, He will meet the hunger and the need I have. They wanted to transition from having head knowledge to having a heart knowledge where they could experience Him.

Mark Russell

Woman with bleeding for 12 years: *(story found in Mark 5:24-34)*

Her plight was awful, she had no hope. Her doctor had given up, it was this or nothing. This was her last hope, but it was hope with a purpose, it was more a question of if only...

Despite the crowds, despite the busyness of town, despite her own position in society, she hoped, no, she was certain that this man would be able to help her. The man was in town, He was in her area, and she knew that she had to reach Him, somehow. She had to make sure that He did not leave town without her having seen Him, without her having touched something of Him, without something of Him having touched her. Stories about this man had gone before Him. This was her chance; she could not let it pass her by. She was at that time in her life when she was desperate.

The man was in town, she knew it would be busy, but it was busier than she imagined. Not only were His followers surrounding Him, it seemed the entire town was too. She knew she could not give up, she knew this had to be her moment. She had no choice, she had to push in.

She pushed, she barged, she was pushed back, but with every step back she went two forward. It was this or nothing. It was a fight she had to win, and there was nothing she could lose. If only she could get close enough, if only a slight connection could be made.

Then it happened, after all the pushing, after all the fighting through, she had her moment. This was it, there was no turning back, there was no second thought. There was no doubt that it would not work, no thought she should give up. This was the moment her desperation had brought her to. All she had to do was reach out, all that needed to happen was make that connection, all she needed to do was touch Him.

In that moment, in that instant, in that split second something happened, the man felt it, she felt it. But to her there was more, to her it was more than a touch, there was power. Her life had been changed, she knew it, she knew that her desperation had been met; she knew her battle was over, she knew her situation was instantly better. Just a moment ago she was so desperate, she had nowhere else to turn, but now, now she had her life back, now she had a story to tell.

The man lowered through the roof: *(taken from Mark 2:1-5)*

It was no use, there was nothing he could do. He had been lying in the same place, he had been reliant on everyone else, and he couldn't even go to the market without help.

As usual his friends, his ever faithful friends, had come to check up on him. They had come to take him for a walk, well, they would walk, he would be carried, to him it was an ordinary day. His friends had heard about a man in town and all they had to do was get their friend in front of Him. They knew the task would be difficult, but they knew it was not impossible. They knew that their friend's life could be changed if only this man could meet Him.

The friends knew the time, they knew the place. What they didn't know was the crowds that were already there, what were they to do? The desperation of the friends grew inside them again, they would not get discouraged, they would not give up; they knew this was the time for their friend. Nothing would stop them, nothing would get in their way of the destiny they sought for their friend; of the freedom they knew could be his. Nothing was going to be impossible for them, they had come this far, they would not give up now.

The friends pressed on with the plan. In the middle of the meeting that had already started, they lowered their friend through the roof. There was no other option, they had made a hole and decided they would interrupt what was going on, this would interrupt the great teacher. This would put their friend where he needed to be in order that he would be noticed by the man. They knew this would be all that was required; this was all that was needed. This would be a life changing encounter.

It worked, the encounter happened, the words were spoken. So few words, but these very words changed the life of their friend, he was free. One simple encounter out of a desperation had changed everything, they had not been tempted to give up, their simple pressing in had been enough.

Two blind men: (taken from Matthew 20:29-34)

Their situation was no different from others around them. They had needs like others, they needed a touch and they needed to see this man. Their problem though, even though they could not see, was that they needed to ensure that the man saw them.

They were not going to be put off by their condition, they had the disadvantage, but they could hear and speak. They had heard the man was coming to town; they were desperate enough to ensure they were at the side of the road where the man would be passing early. They were determined enough to do what was required; they would shout if needed, all they needed was to get the man's attention.

It was time. They heard the crowd even though they could not see. They knew the crowd was large, they knew it would take something special in order for the man to see them. They shouted, they shouted His name, they called on Him, and they called on the name that would change their life if only He heard them. Things were not going well, they shouted, but they were being told to keep quiet. They knew despite the noise around them that they were being heard but not by the man they desperately needed to be heard by.

The two men were not going to be put off. They were not going to give up, they would persevere. It could have been so easy to give up, it could have been so easy to admit defeat, but they were desperate. They would not allow the noise around them to defeat them; they knew the time was still now. They could not see, but they still had their voices, they were willing to lose this too, this was their only chance. They had to ensure the man would see them; they had to ensure they won the attention of this man. It didn't matter how long for, they knew this man could change their lives if only they got His attention.

They shouted louder, they declared His name with greater volume. They did all they could for this man to hear them above the noise around.

Then it happened, the man spoke, the crowd were silenced. They had succeeded, they had His attention. He had stopped, more than that He talked to them. They were now able to speak directly to Him. They were able to explain what they wanted, they had known that His attention would be enough, but to be asked specifically what they wanted was more than they imagined. They now knew the attention of the man was fully theirs. They knew at that moment their lives would be changed. They knew their perseverance had paid off, this would be the moment they would never be the same again.

How desperate are we? Are we in that place where we just want and need an encounter? Are we desperate enough to risk it all in order that we grab the attention of the man, the King, the Lord, our Father?

Are we desperate enough where we are willing to persevere, despite the struggles and opposition? Are we desperate enough to push in and press on in order that the one thing we seek, the one thing we need, is a life changing meeting. Because we know a life changing touch will be all that is required.

No matter what the cost, are we desperate enough to seek Him? Are we desperate enough to be intimate with Him? Are we hungering after such intimacy with Him, that we know that only He is enough?

Being Face to Face with Him

I believe the second step to intimacy with the Father is being face to face with Him, just as we saw with Moses. Once we have a desperation for Him, then we can begin to see Him face to face. We can behold His beauty, we can see the love He has for us in His eyes and we can experience more of Him.

> *"The LORD would speak to Moses face to face, as a man speaks with his friend"*
>
> *Exodus 33:11*

A person's face is a physical representation of that person. By looking at the face of a person we are able to know who that person is; we generally distinguish people by looking at their face. The face is the part that identifies who they are.

To have a face-to-face conversation with someone provides an opportunity for there to be an intimate connection. Sometimes a face to face encounter will facilitate the ability to gain a complete understanding between the two. Just as Moses had those times with God, so it is true with us, we need to develop encounters with God. We need to treasure those encounters. To be face to face with God is seeking to be alone with Him, having no distractions, just you and Him. We have the promise in James:

> *"Come near to God and He will come near to you"*
>
> *James 4:8*

Also in Jeremiah we read:

> *"You will seek me and find me when you seek me with all your heart."*
>
> *Jeremiah 29:13*

Seeking His face or having a face to face encounter is to seek His presence, because God's face represents His very nature. God's face is the essence of who He is; it represents His person and His presence. So to seek the face of God is to seek intimacy with Him.

You can only develop intimacy with someone when you spend time in their presence, we can only develop intimacy with Him when we spend time in His presence.

Being Unashamed

The third step to intimacy is to not be ashamed. We read in Jeremiah 9:24 that we can boast that we understand and know Father. To boast about is speak openly and proudly, in other words we are not ashamed of our relationship with Father, we have such a freedom and peace we want to shout it from the rooftops. There is nothing better than being in an intimate relationship with Him. I proudly wear my wedding ring. It boasts and declares I am married, but only when I tell people, only the action of how I am with my wife can people see the joy and the love I have for her.

Obedience

We saw in Genesis that obedience to Him is an important step to intimacy. The relationship was broken between Father and Adam due to the disobedience of Adam. The obedience we are talking about here is not out of fear, but out of a love for Him. We obey because we are in relationship, not because of any fear of reprimand or duty. As we obey and follow Him, we begin to realise that He always looks out for our best, He works for our good. It is only as we walk in obedience with Him that we see His love for us. We gain greater revelation of God as our Father, how He sees us, and that in itself brings us deeper into Him.

Disobedience is an act of rebellion, it suggests I don't need God, I know better. Of course that thought is the complete opposite of intimacy. Where there is true intimacy with Him, we both know and experience Him and therefore we would understand how pointless it is to say "I don't need God". Disobedience is also a form of idolatry which is to consider something of a greater value or love something more than God. Clearly if we love something more than Him, we are not demonstrating an intimate relationship with Him. My relationship with my wife is such that I know her. I know how she thinks and what her likes and dislikes are, this has happened over the years we have been married because I have chosen to love her above all else.

Sacrifice

The final step I want to look at which will help lead us into intimacy with the Father is the sacrifice we make for Him. We saw Paul's sacrifice. He was willing to give up everything in order that he might know Christ. Jesus ultimately sacrificed

Himself that we might know the Father. Are we willing to give up everything that we might know Him better? That we might be more intimate with Him? If we are willing to give all of who we are, we receive something far greater; all of who He is.

You might be reading this and thinking "I have tried this I don't seem to be able to reach this level of intimacy". It should be understood that striving and willing ourselves to make it happen is not the answer.

Hindrances

At times we may feel that we are struggling with enjoying increasing intimacy with Father. Sometimes painful childhood experiences can lead us to put up walls of protection around our hearts without us realising we have done so. This in turn may hinder our intimacy with Father.

There may be others who for whatever reason have learnt to become independent or become self-reliant, which in turn may make it more difficult to become fully dependent and reliant upon Father. In the chapter 'Co-heirs with Christ' I talked about the orphan heart and referred to the twenty characteristics the orphan heart carries according to Jack Frost, all of which could affect our level of intimacy with Father.

The good news is we are not in a black hole with no way out. We can experience breakthrough; we can experience healing. We may need to forgive someone who has hurt us or we may believe a lie that needs to be replaced with His truth. If you feel you are struggling with pursuing intimacy with Father maybe consider a ministry such as Bethel Sozo to allow Father to highlight and heal any areas that are affecting you in this area.

Intimacy is not something that is difficult to attain, it is not out of reach. The Father has made it possible for each one of us to experience intimacy with Him because that was the reason we were created and that is why we are created in His image, that we might have and experience intimacy with Him.

Prayer:

Father I thank You that You have made it possible to experience intimacy with You. From this day forward I want to experience a more intimate relationship, I want to know You more. I want to come face to face with You; I want an encounter with Your presence that I might not be the same again. I thank You that as I seek You I will find You. I am willing to do what it takes to have an intimate relationship with You, My loving Father.

Inheritance

"And you also were included in Christ when you heard the message of truth, the gospel of your salvation. When you believed, you were marked in Him with a seal, the promised Holy Spirit, who is a deposit guaranteeing our inheritance until the redemption of those who are God's possession—to the praise of his glory."

Ephesians 1: 13-14

In the natural an inheritance is usually something that is passed down from one generation to another and normally after the passing away of the older. It is something that the older generation has but wishes to pass on to the next generation. It is in essence a helping hand. For example, when my Mum passed away she left me a sum of money. It was a helping hand for me; I did nothing to receive it except of course be her son. I also did not have to pay for it, it was money that she had earned over the years, but it was given to me freely.

Mark Gyde says in his book 'A Father to You':

> *"An inheritance is a valuable thing. It is far more than the sum of the goods or monetary value passed from one generation to the next. It represents someone's life and work, his or her very soul. It is not something to be taken lightly or squandered. An inheritance truly is a treasure."* [1]

According to the Old Testament an inheritance is a birthright; it is something that is handed down only to the older son. If you were the first-born son of a Jewish family, you received a double portion of your family's inheritance. You received at least twice as much as any other family member.

> *"If a man has two wives, and he loves one but not the other, and both bear him sons but the firstborn is the son of the wife he does not love, when he wills his property to his sons, he must not give the rights of the firstborn to the son of the wife he loves in preference to his actual firstborn, the son of the wife he does not love. He must acknowledge the son of his unloved wife as the firstborn by giving him a double share of all he has. That son is the first sign of his father's strength. The right of the firstborn belongs to him."*
>
> *Deuteronomy 21:15-17*

We see here this thought being explained, the firstborn must receive a double share, it is a passing down of what the father has. When we read the account of Jacob and Esau we see more clearly this importance.

> *"Jacob replied, "First sell me your birthright." "Look, I am about to die," Esau said. "What good is the birthright to me?" But Jacob said, "Swear to me first." So he swore an oath to him, selling his birthright to Jacob."*
>
> *Genesis 25:31-33*

---

[1] Gyde, M. (2011) *A Father to You.* p.72. (Permission granted)

Jacob was the younger son. He knew the importance of receiving the birthright, however, he also knew it was not his to receive. Since he knew the inheritance had significance he did all he could to obtain it, that which ordinarily would not have been his, and so he forced Esau to sell his birthright to him.

Even in today's society we can see the importance of receiving an inheritance. Today's inheritance is not limited to the first born son and does not have to stay within the family. However, to receive an inheritance is a good thing. It is possible to receive an inheritance but not actually draw from it, not actually use it. I mentioned earlier the inheritance I received when my mother died. At that time both mine and my wife's cars were becoming unreliable. We could have chosen to ignore the inheritance received and continue to struggle with the cars we had, but we chose to use the inheritance to help us out. An inheritance is something that should be used to help. It is a head start in life, it is a free gift. We have seen that a birthright in the Old Testament was an honour to receive, and always used to help out the next generation. It was such a significant thing that, as we saw with the example of Jacob and Esau, people fought over it.

So, do we all have an inheritance? If so, what does it look like? What is our spiritual inheritance?

Let's look at a passage in Deuteronomy:

> *"But as for you, the LORD took you and brought you out of the iron smelting furnace, out of Egypt, to be the people of His inheritance, as you are now"*
>
> *Deuteronomy 4:20*

We see that the Lord brought His people out of Egypt in order that they might be able to receive His inheritance. It is the same with us. The Father saw the plight we were in, He saw the trouble, and has made it possible through Jesus for us to now be the people of His inheritance; a people who can receive His inheritance.

We are the people of His inheritance. Jesus has made it possible by His blood that we might receive it. Because of the death and resurrection of Jesus we have already received our inheritance. He has paid the price for us and we now have permission to possess what is rightfully ours.

"How much more then, will the blood of Christ, who through the eternal Spirit offered Himself unblemished to God, cleanse our consciences from acts that lead to death, so that we may serve the living God. For this reason Christ, is the mediator of a new covenant, that those who are called may receive the promised eternal inheritance – now that He has died as a ransom to set them free from the sins committed under the first covenant."

Hebrews 9:14-15

It is because of the work of the cross that we are able to receive any inheritance from God. In fact, we read in this passage that our inheritance from Him is a promise. We know that in Him all His promises are yes and amen (2 Corinthians 1:20). We read in the book of Joshua:

"Not one of all the LORD'S good promises to the house of Israel failed; everyone was fulfilled."

Joshua 21:45

Each and everyone one of God's children receives a great eternal inheritance. Jesus is the only Son of God and He receives the inheritance, but all that Jesus has we receive also.

The Apostle Paul writes:

"In Him also we have obtained an inheritance, being predestined according to the purpose of Him who works all things according to the counsel of His will."

Ephesians 1:11 (NKJV)

It has always been the purpose of God to include all believers in the inheritance that Christ has won and paid the price for us to receive. Our inheritance is free, we do not have to pay for it. Notice also that Paul uses the past tense, we have received it. It is ours now to take ownership of. It could be described as being in our spiritual bank accounts; we are able to draw on it now. So often people do not live as though they have received an inheritance. They live as though it is something they can obtain later when they die and go to Heaven. The truth is, we have access to part of our inheritance now, it is not something we have to wait for.

"And you also were included in Christ when you heard the message of truth, the gospel of your salvation. When you believed, you were marked in Him with a seal, the promised Holy Spirit, who is a deposit guaranteeing our inheritance until the redemption of those who are God's possession—to the praise of His glory."

Ephesians 1:13-14

The Holy Spirit is a deposit. He has marked us to be able to receive this inheritance, which according to Paul is at the redemption of our bodies. However, that does not mean we do not have access to that inheritance now, it does not mean that we are unable to draw from it today. We were included when we heard the truth, when we received Jesus. It was at that moment that we became heirs of God and co-heirs of Christ (Romans 8:17). It was in that moment we become partakers of the inheritance He has for us.

An inheritance is something that is given to us that previously we did not possess. But our inheritance in Him has now been revealed and therefore we have permission to possess it.

Sometimes inheritances are put into a trust. This could be because the recipient is too young or too immature to be able take responsibility for what has been handed down to them. These trusts are a secure place; no one can touch the contents of the trust until the recipient is mature enough. This is usually when the recipient of the inheritance reaches a certain age when he or she is able to steward the inheritance given to them in a right and proper way.[2]

Paul in Galatians has the same thought:

"What I am saying is this as long as the heir is a child, he is no different from a slave, although he owns the whole estate. He is subject to the guardians and trustees until the time is set by his father."

Galatians 4:1-2

The word used for child here is referring to a child who is not fully grown up, a minor. In the UK the legal driving age is 17.

---

[2] Jack Frost in his book 'Spiritual Slavery to Spiritual Sonship' has much more to say on this whole subject of receiving our inheritance as immature believers. He gives nine reasons why receiving our full inheritance as immature believers is dangerous. p.108-110.

Prior to the child turning 17 the child is not considered mature enough to be able to adequately handle the dangers and responsibilities that come with driving a car.

I heard a great example that illustrates this; a couple had a son, the son would have full access to their house. He would be able to come and go, he would be able to roam throughout the house, but depending on his maturity (or his age) there would be certain things that he would not get complete access too. For example, the kitchen. There are certain things that would be dangerous for him unless he was accompanied by his parents. As he gets older, only then would he be able to access freely and use all things in the kitchen.

In order to understand this more fully let us recognise that part of our inheritance is our salvation. We are saved because of our acceptance of Jesus as our Saviour. However, our inheritance is so much more than just salvation; salvation is just the beginning of the journey to receiving it. Our inheritance is all that Jesus has won for us. Just as Jesus received everything the Father has and so do we. All that Jesus has we also have.

We are required to steward what we have been given. It is our responsibility to use all that we have well; we are to grow into maturity to be able handle what we have been given. We are to grow in our walk in Him. One way we can learn to steward that which we have been given by the Father is to be in close relationship with Him and know His heart. This involves living from the inheritance and not living for it. When we live for something we are living in order to receive, rather than recognising we already have it. Once we do this we can begin to take responsibility for what we have received. Just as an earthly heir has not yet fully been given all that is his, he does still own it. Take the example of the British royal family. The Prince of Wales is the heir to the throne. He will fully take his place when the Queen passes away, but in the meantime he still carries out the duties of the crown. He carries out his duties as a member of the royal family, he does not sit around waiting for such a time as he becomes King. He takes responsibility for who he is and what he has now. It is the same with us. As heirs of God we own the treasures of the Kingdom of God. These treasures are in our 'account' until the appointed time to receive the fullness of. Even though we have not yet entered into the kingdom with our resurrected bodies, because of the Spirit who is our deposit, we can begin to experience and enjoy some of those treasures right here, right now. We are required to steward what we already have in order that we demonstrate we are able to responsibly handle more. As we become more mature, we steward well and then we are entrusted to receive more.

Like any inheritance you receive when someone dies, so it is true here, someone has to die in order to receive its fullness. Christ died so that we can receive in part now but fully as we continue to grow in maturity. Until that time we would not be able to handle all the fullness of our inheritance. We will share in the eternal glory of the Kingdom of God, no one can take that away from us. No one can take our inheritance from us, it is legally ours, it has our name on it and it is final. We can enjoy in part now, because of the deposit of the Holy Spirt, and as we mature we can continue to draw on all that we have received.

Before we look in more depth at what our spiritual inheritance is, let us spend a bit of time understanding the features of it.

> *"Praise be to the God and Father of our Lord Jesus Christ! In His great mercy He has given us new birth into a living hope through the resurrection of Jesus Christ from the dead, and into an inheritance that can never perish, spoil or fade – kept in Heaven for you"*
>
> 1 Peter 1:3-4

As we saw earlier in this chapter we receive an inheritance when someone has died. Our inheritance is because of the death of Jesus, it is stored in Heaven, not so that it is untouchable, but more as a place of security. According to Peter our inheritance has four major characteristics:

Imperishable

If we receive an earthy inheritance, for example a car, over time if the car is not maintained it will begin to perish. Our spiritual inheritance is not subject to the normal laws, it is kept in Heaven, where moth and rust do not destroy (Matthew 6:19). Our inheritance is imperishable.

Unspoiled

All we receive in Christ, including our spiritual inheritance, is perfect. After all Jesus is holy, He is blameless, He is pure, He is exalted above the Heavens (Hebrews 7:26). As our inheritance is in Him it stands to reason that our inheritance has the same characteristics. There is no earthy corruption or weakness that can touch what God has granted for us. There is nothing on earth that is not flawed. There is nothing on earth that is perfect. Everything therefore, on earth, is at some point in time going to spoil and become imperfect. As our inheritance is stored in Heaven it will always remain perfect and unspoiled.

Unfading

In Malawi there is both a dry season and a wet season both of which have their beauty. The rainy season brings a vibrancy of colour; the dry and dusty land comes to life and the landscape gets its colour back. However, during the dry season because of the lack of rain the ground dries up, the grass fades in colour, and you notice the landscape change as the colour fades. I remember once returning to Malawi after a short break away and noticing how the land had become lush and green with the rains. Our inheritance in Christ is not something that is going to fade over time, our inheritance has the rain of God over it; it never diminishes in colour or value or beauty. Our inheritance is unfading.

Reserved

Our inheritance is reserved. We read earlier that the Holy Spirit is a deposit. When we put a deposit down on something it means that that item has become ours, we are now the owners. No one can take that from us, it is awaiting the time when it has been paid for in full.

> *"He anointed us, set His seal of ownership on us, and put His Spirit in our hearts as a deposit, guaranteeing what is to come."*
>
> *2 Corinthians 1:21b-22*

When we buy a house, we pay a deposit. The house legally belongs to us; we have full ownership of it. However, most people cannot afford to buy a house outright, so you will arrange a mortgage, you will have an agreement that a mortgage company will put down the rest of the finance. Over time you pay off the mortgage and the debt becomes smaller. The house is legally yours, you are free to do with it as you please, but if you were to sell the house later, the mortgage company would receive their share of the unpaid mortgage.

With the death of Jesus, we have received our inheritance. He has paid the price for us and we now have permission to possess what is rightfully ours. Whilst everything has been done and fully paid for it is only as we become mature in Him that we can draw on that which is in our spiritual bank account.

Our inheritance is a glorious one, it is something we should be thankful to receive. It is an honour. It is our birthright. It is a free gift given to each one of us.

We have looked at the four main characteristics of our inheritance, and understood that our inheritance includes salvation. I believe however, it is so much more than that, in fact, who we are in Him is part of our inheritance. I want to take a moment to look at the life of Elisha and see if there are some things about his life that we too should be able to experience in the here and now as part of our inheritance.

> *"When they had crossed, Elijah said to Elisha, "Tell me what I can do for you before I am taken away from you?" "Let me inherit a double portion of your spirit," Elisha replied. "You have asked a difficult thing," Elijah said, "yet if you see me when I am taken from you, it will be yours – otherwise not.""*
>
> *2 Kings 2:9-10*

We saw at the beginning of this chapter that in Elisha's time inheritance was a birthright of the firstborn son who received a double portion. We see in this passage from 2 Kings that Elisha wanted to "inherit a double portion" of Elijah's spirit.

Elisha was not the firstborn of Elijah, hence why it was difficult for Elijah to grant, according to tradition this was not even possible. But notice Elijah says "if you are with me when I am taken from you, it will be yours." The question for Elijah was actually how hungry is Elisha? How hungry are we to receive? Are we ready to move into a greater inheritance that is rightfully ours today?

The life of Elisha was one of complete surrender:

"Elijah went up to him [Elisha] and threw his cloak around him. Elisha then left his oxen and ran after Elijah. "Let me kiss my father and mother good-bye," he said, "and then I will come with you." "Go back," Elijah replied. "What have I done to you?" So Elisha left him and went back. He took his yoke of oxen and slaughtered them. He burned the ploughing equipment to cook the meat and gave it to the people, and they ate. Then he set out to follow Elijah and became his attendant."

1 Kings 19:20-21

Elisha was willing to give up everything to follow Elijah; he was in a place of wanting to receive a double portion. Jesus wants the same for each one of us; He wants us to be in complete surrender to Him. We are to be totally given up to Him, just as Jesus says:

""If anyone would come after me, he must deny himself and take up his cross and follow me""

Matthew 16:24

Our inheritance is in Him. Our inheritance is far better than we could imagine, our inheritance is of greater value than the life we have on earth. When we moved to Malawi we sold and gave up all that we owned in the UK. I share this to show that at times that is what is required to be able to move into the inheritance He has for each one of us. At times we are required to give up everything, knowing that what is coming is greater. Of course that is not the reason we give up what we have, because remember we come *from* a place of inheritance and not *for* it.

The question for us is how hungry are we to be able to draw upon the resources of Heaven, our inheritance? I believe, just as Elisha received a double portion, we too can experience life in all its fullness. Just as Elisha's life was a great one, because of our inheritance, ours too can be the same.

What was the effect of the double portion on Elisha's life? He was able to lead a triumphant life, a life of victory. We too, with the Holy Spirit, can lead a triumphant and victorious life.

Let's spend some time looking at four different aspects of Elisha's life and his inheritance:

Spiritual Equipment

> *"He picked up the cloak that had fallen from Elijah and went back and stood on the back of the Jordan. Then he took the cloak that had fallen from him and struck the water with it. "Where now is the LORD, the God of Elijah?" he asked. When he struck the water, it divided to the right and to the left, and he crossed over."*
>
> *2 Kings 2:13-14*

Elisha had a mantle which was the cloak that he wore. This mantle was like an anointing, it was a spiritual tool that he used to enable him to perform many miracles. We too have the same tool at our disposal, we too have such an anointing ,and this anointing is also part of our inheritance. As we saw earlier the idea of an inheritance is to help us move forward. We are anointed by the Holy Spirit to help us as we live our lives for Him.

"But you will receive power when the Holy Spirit comes on you; and you will be my witnesses in Jerusalem and in all Judea, and Samaria, and to the end of the earth."

Acts 1:8

We have received the Holy Spirit who is power. This power is to help us to represent the Father.

Also we read:

"As for you, the anointing you received from Him remains in you, and you do not need anyone to teach you. But as His anointing teaches you about all things and as that anointing is real, not counterfeit - just as it was taught you, remain in Him."

1 John 2:27

The anointing we receive is from the Holy Spirit. The Holy Spirit living in each one of us is a part of our inheritance. We have been given the Holy Spirit to help us in all things. Not just for works of power but also to remind us of the things Jesus taught us. It is sad that there are people who do not believe that the Holy Spirit is for today, or others that do not see the importance of the work of the Spirit in our lives. I believe these people are missing out on an important aspect of who they are, they are missing out on part of their inheritance as a child of God.

Just as Elisha had a cloak, I believe that we too have a cloak; the cloak of the Holy Spirit. Just as Elisha received this cloak as part of his inheritance, so too have we received the cloak as part of our inheritance. The Holy Spirit is a part of our inheritance as children of God. Jesus said we will do greater things than He (John 1:50), we can only do these greater things through the power of the Spirit.

Living by the spirit

"When the servant of the man of God got up and went out early the next morning, an army with horses and chariots had surrounded the city. "Oh my lord, what shall we do?" the servant asked. "Don't be afraid," the prophet answered. "Those who are with us are more that those who are with them.""

2 Kings 6:15-16

Elisha was a man who lived by the Spirit; he was a man who was not afraid. Even when things were too great or too difficult, by living in the Spirit he was able to stay calm. He was able to see things beyond the natural.

Part of our inheritance due to the Spirit dwelling inside of us is that we, like Elisha, can and should live by the Spirit:

"Since we live by the Spirit, let us keep in step with the Spirit."

Galatians 5:25

Paul teaches here that because we live by the Spirit, we can keep in step with the Spirit. It is the Holy Spirit that enables us to live the way we should. We are empowered by the Spirit to live a life without fear, for God has not given us a spirit of fear (2 Timothy 1:7 NKJV). We are empowered by the Spirit to live a life of freedom, to live as Elisha did and see beyond the natural, and see things as God sees them. We too are enabled by living by the Spirit to live in rest. Just as Jesus lived from a place of rest, this is for us too; we can live from a place of rest.

Man of Spiritual Vision

"And Elisha prayed, "O LORD, open his eyes so he may see." Then the LORD opened the servant's eyes, and he looked and saw the hills full of horses and chariots of fire around Elisha."

2 Kings 6:17

Not only did Elisha live by the Spirit but in doing so he was a man with vision, he was able to see what in the natural was impossible to see. It was part of the inherited double portion he received from Elijah.

"He will bring glory to me by taking from what is mine and making it known to you. All that belongs to the Father is mine. That is why I said the Spirit will take from what is mine and make it known to you."

John 16:14-15

Jesus teaches us that the Holy Spirit will do the same for us. When we are uncertain and feel we do not have a clear path and can't see clearly, through the Holy Spirit that dwells within us we will be able to see what others can't.

Have you ever been in a position where you just don't know what to do? Life has seemingly become impossible; it appears that no matter what you do it's going to be the wrong thing, nothing is going to work out?

Just before we moved to Malawi we were in a similar position. All was going well, we had sold our house, we were set to hand in our notices at work and then the plans we had made appeared to fall through. We both knew that our move to Malawi was the right one, but it appeared now that our transition was not going as well. It was during this time that I received a vision; I saw two angels in a boxing match, one was dressed in white and the other dressed in black. The match was even, it appeared as though the match would be drawn. But then I saw Jesus ride in on a white horse and suddenly the angel in black was laid on the floor with a foot of Jesus resting on him in a position of victory. Whilst this was not a vision of how to overcome the problem, it was a vision of peace. I saw that Jesus had the victory in this situation and that despite the circumstances in the natural, I knew that in the spiritual it had already been won. I was able to see beyond what the natural said was becoming impossible, to see that in the spiritual Jesus was fighting for us and therefore the impossible would become possible.

Part of our inheritance is being able to recognise that what we see in the natural realm is not always how they are in the spiritual. It provides us with peace.

> *"Peace I leave with you; my peace I give you. I do not give to you as the world gives. Do not let your hearts be troubled and do not be afraid"*
>
> *John 14:27*

It is only when we tap into our inheritance to see things as they are that we are able to live in that peace. When we live from the realm of the Kingdom and see things as they are, only then are we able to overcome. We are not meant to live in defeat, that is not who we are, we live a life of the Spirit, and therefore we live a life of freedom and victory.

Died a victorious death

> *"Now Elisha was suffering from the illness from which he died. Jehoash king of Israel went down to see him and wept over him. "My father! My father!" he cried. "The chariots and horsemen of Israel!" Elisha said, "Get a bow and some arrows," and he did so. "Take the bow in your hands," he said to the king of Israel. When he had taken it, Elisha put his hands on the king's hands. "Open the east window," he said, and he opened it. "Shoot!" Elisha said, and he shot. "The LORD'S arrows of victory, the arrow of victory over Aram!" Elisha declared. "You will completely destroy the Arameans at Apheck.""*
>
> *2 Kings 13:14-17*

The final aspect of Elisha's story is that even on his death bed he was victorious; he was able to lead the king to victory.

Just as in the previous three aspects of Elisha's life we have looked at, just as these were all part of his inherited double portion, so too is this final one; we too are victorious in our death.

> *"For everyone born of God overcomes the world. This is the victory that has overcome the world, even our faith. Who is it that overcomes the world? Only he who believes that Jesus is the Son of God."*
>
> *1 John 5:4-5*

We have the victory in Jesus, He is the one in whom we have the victory. Part of our spiritual inheritance is the victory we have over sin, the victory we have over the devil, the victory we have over death.

> *"Death has been swallowed up in victory. ... The sting of death in sin, and the power of sin is the law. But thanks be to God! He gives us the victory through our Lord Jesus Christ."*
>
> *1 Corinthians 15:54 & 56-57*

We have the victory; it is ours by inheritance through Jesus. It is time to look upwards; it is time that we as His children walk in that victory. It is time to realise that everything we have has been purchased for us at the cross. We do not have to wait to draw on the victory we have, we can call on that victory now. We are no longer slaves to our old way of life, that life has been put to death. We should be walking in the inheritance that is rightfully ours.

The inheritance we receive is given freely to us through Jesus and all that was His (by right), He gives to us through grace, by His Spirit.

We have received an inheritance; we have received a double portion, the Holy Spirit. The inheritance we have received will impact our lives. Our inheritance is not to be wasted, and our inheritance is partly received now. The inheritance we have received now, however, is not only for our benefit, it is for the benefit of others. The inheritance we have now, the Holy Spirit, is to enable and empower us to make a difference in other people's lives. Just as an inheritance is to be a helping hand, our inheritance is a helping hand for others too. Our spiritual inheritance is to bring Heaven here on earth. What does that mean? It simply means that what we expect in Heaven, we too can expect here on earth. Or as Bill Johnson says:

> *"A spiritual inheritance is about making us more effective and efficient in our representation of the King and his kingdom. It's not for our gratification."*[3]

Good news, not only has Jesus done everything possible for us to receive eternal life, He has done everything possible for us to live the life to be able to represent the Kingdom here on earth.

Prayer:

Father I thank You for the inheritance we have in You. Thank You the inheritance is not something we have to wait for, but it is rightfully ours now. Father I ask that I continue to walk into my inheritance and as that is a blessing for me, I ask that I might be able to represent Your Kingdom to others, that I might be able to benefit others with the inheritance I have. I ask Father that I might steward well today what I have and in doing so others will be blessed.

---

[3] Johnson, B. (2005) *The Supernatural Power of a Transformed Mind*. Destiny Image. p.154. (Permission granted)

Mark Russell

Chosen

"In Him we were also chosen, having been predestined according to the plan of Him who works out everything in conformity with the purpose of His will."

Ephesians 1:11

"But you are a chosen race, a royal priesthood, a holy nation, a people for His own possession, that you may proclaim the excellences of Him who called you out of darkness into His marvellous light."

1 Peter 2:9 (ESV)

Have you ever been involved in sports and had the agonising wait as you line up for the team captains to pick their side? I am sure like me, if that was the case you knew the captains always wanted the best players on their team and therefore they always picked the best first. Maybe you were one of the best and you were picked first. Or second. On the other hand maybe you were the other end of the scale, your sporting skills didn't match those who were picked first and you found yourself being picked with the last few. What did that feel like? Did you feel inadequate?

How about when you do your food shopping? You are at the fruit and vegetable section and I am sure you hand pick the best fruit and vegetables available, you only want the best. He only wants the best for us!

Within the New Testament one of the messages that comes through is that we are chosen. I don't believe that these passages are referring to God choosing individuals to be saved or not. God loves all of mankind, He died for all to receive Him, He wants everyone to come to Him. But rather I suggest that these passages are referring to the Church, that God chooses His church. It is within the context of church we are chosen. To go back to the team analogy, His team is His church and we each have our part to play as we partner with Him. He chooses each one of us to be on His winning team.

When we read the passage from 1 Peter:

"But you are a chosen race, a royal priesthood, a holy nation, a people for His own possession, that you may proclaim the excellences of Him who called you out of darkness into His marvellous light."

1 Peter 2:9 (ESV)

We are reading that we have been hand-picked. He chose us not because we are all that was left, there was no other choice, or there was nothing better. But because we have all that is required of us, He wants us on His team. Simply put He loves us. We have been chosen by Him for a purpose. (I will discuss this later in this chapter). In fact, we have been chosen for His inheritance (Psalm 33:12). He has given Himself to you and I.

If you receive an inheritance it would normally be of some worth or value. Maybe it is a sum of money, a property, a family heirloom; whatever it is it becomes special to the recipient.

Let us have a look at that same verse in 1 Peter from The New King James version and The Passion Translation:

*"But you are a chosen generation, a royal priesthood, a holy nation, **His own special people**, that you may proclaim the praises of Him who called you out of darkness in His marvellous light…"*

1 Peter 2:9 (NKJV, emphasis added)

*"But you are God's **chosen treasure** – priests who are kings, a spiritual nation set apart as God's devoted ones. He called you out of darkness to experience His marvellous light…"*

1 Peter 2:9 (TPT, emphasis added)

Notice we are not just chosen for His own possession but we are chosen because we are a special people, we are special to God. We, His church, are His treasure. Have you ever thought of yourself as special? Have you ever considered yourself to be a treasure? No matter what your answer, no matter how you see yourself, God sees you as special; He thinks highly of you, He calls you a treasure -- you have value. So much so that Jesus says we now belong to Him:

"If you belonged to the world, it would love you as its own. As it is, you do not belong to the world, but I have chosen you out of the world."

John 15:19a

We have been chosen out of this world and our citizenship is now in Heaven (Philippians 3:20). We belong to Him, we have been chosen by Him for His team to play for His Kingdom, and we are so special to Him that we are given a new home. We are no longer part of this world and we have been chosen "out of" this world. Just as when you choose a piece of fruit, you remove it from the display and put it into your ownership. We have been chosen, we belong to Him and therefore we have been taken out of the world. This world is no longer our home; our home is now with Him in His kingdom. But even more than that, Paul says we are seated with Him in Heavenly places (Ephesians 2:6). We have not just been taken from this world, but we now have a new home with Him and we are now seated with Him.

Perhaps your answer to the earlier question *"Do you see yourself as special?"* was no, I don't see myself as special. Maybe you don't have a high opinion of yourself and you think you're not special, why would God choose me, I'm not worth it? Let's look at what Paul is saying to the Corinthian church for a moment.

> *"Brothers, think of what you were when you were called. Not many of you were wise by human standards; not many were influential; not many were of noble birth. But God chose the foolish things of the world to shame the wise; God chose the weak things to shame the strong. He chose the lowly things of this world and the despised things – and the things that are not – to nullify the things that are, so that no one may boast before Him."*
>
> *1 Corinthians 1:26-29*

He has chosen you. He chose me. He has chosen us from where we were, a place of sin. He saw our defects but still He selected us, He still hand-picked us. It does not matter to Him where we have come from, it does not matter to Him our level of intellect. For Him our skills and abilities are not a factor, whether we are weak or strong. It does not even matter to Him what our class and standing in society is. He chose us despite our circumstances and despite how we see ourselves, we are still chosen. Regardless of how others see us, in fact no matter how others see us or we see ourselves, He sees us through a different lens. It does not matter to Him if we were picked last for the sports event. No matter what we perceive our inadequacies to be, He does not see them. He sees us as perfect.

The Bible is full of characters that in the worldly sense would not have been an obvious choice. For example, Abraham was old (Genesis 24:1), Jeremiah thought he was too young (Jeremiah 1:7), the same was true of Timothy (1 Timothy 4:12). King David was an adulterer (2 Samuel 11:1-27) and Paul murdered followers of Jesus (Acts 9:1-5).

However, notice what Paul teaches:

> *"For He chose us in Him before the creation of the world…"*
>
> *Ephesians 1:4*

And also

> *"While we were still sinners Christ died for us."*
>
> *Romans 5:8*

He saw what we were, but He also sees who we are. He sees that we do have value; He sees that we do have potential. Notice too from the passage in 1 Corinthians 1 the reason: "So that no one may boast." We are who we are because of Him.

It is not through our own effort, it is not because of anyone other than Him.

Partnership

Throughout my time living in Malawi I learnt many lessons. One of these is that God does not need us, He does not need me. He created me from nothing, so it is obvious He does not need me. So why are we called? I believe we are called because He chooses to partner with us. Bill Johnson says:

> *"Everything He's called me to do, He can do better—infinitely better. It's become apparent that He did not choose me for what I can do for Him. He chose me because He loves me".*[1]

He can do so much more than me and He can do it so much better than me, so it stands to reason that He does not *need* me. He chooses me first and foremost because He loves me, but He also wants me to co-labour and partner with Him.

The idea of partnering with Him can be seen in the following passage:

> *"Therefore, holy brothers, **who share** in the Heavenly calling, fix your thoughts on Jesus, the apostle and high priest whom we confess."*
>
> Hebrews 3:1 (emphasis added)

Let us also look at the King James Version:

---

[1] Johnson, B. *Dreaming with God.* Available at: https://www.destinyimage.com/blog/2017/07/13/bill-johnson-dreaming-with-god (Accessed 27th February 2018) (Permission granted)

> *"Therefore, holy brethren, **partakers** of the heavenly calling, consider the Apostle and High Priest of our profession, Christ Jesus"*
>
> Hebrews 3:1 (KJV emphasis added)

As we can see from these two versions, the phrase "who share" has a deeper meaning. It means to partake, literally we take part in the work of Heaven. Therefore we have been chosen by Him to be partners with Christ. If ever you question if you are worthy, just remind yourself of that fact, we are partners with Christ. Not just His servants, not just a people who do His bidding, who work for Him, but we actually work with Him.

When we are in our places of work, employed by others, we work for the manager whoever that may be, and we do whatever is asked of us. In my time being employed I have often been described by my immediate manager as their 'right hand man' meaning that I work with them, rather than just working for them. We were both working for the same goal. So it is true in our calling from God, we are called and chosen to work with Him; we are partners with Him. Through Christ, we have been chosen to partake, or partner with Him. Or as Paul says in 1 Corinthians

> *"For we are co-workers in God's service; you are God's field, God's building."*
>
> 1 Corinthians 3:9

Purpose

So what is the purpose and reason we are called to partner with Him? We understand that we have been given a Commission (Matthew 28:18-19), but often people can have the false idea that we are being left alone, we have been told what to do and it is now our job to get on with it. However, I do not believe that is the case. The next verse in Matthew says:

> *"'And surely I am with you always to the very end of the age.'"*
>
> *Matthew 28:20b*

We can see clearly that just as we have been given a commission, so too are we given everything possible to fulfil that. We also read in the book of Acts:

> *"Do not leave Jerusalem, but wait for the gift my Father promised, which you have heard me speak about. For John baptised with water, but in a few days you will be baptised with the Holy Spirit… But you will receive power when the Holy Spirit comes upon you; and you will be my witnesses in Jerusalem, and in all Judea, and Samaria, and to the ends of the earth"*
>
> *Acts 1:4-5 and 8*

The disciples are told clearly by Jesus in this passage to wait and they will be baptised with the Holy Spirit, and just a few verses later we are told they will receive power. I believe that not only do we know what our purpose is but we really do have everything we need. We have the power of the Holy Spirit, the same power that was at work in Jesus living inside of us, and therefore what more do we need?

So, what are we partnering with Him to do? What is the purpose of this partnership? What is our primary mission?

Our mission, I believe, is to demonstrate something of the Kingdom of God to those around us. I believe this is part of the mandate for us to partner with Him in the purpose He has for us or as Bill Johnson suggests:

> *"In reality, it isn't possible to prove the will of God on earth as it is in Heaven unless we are completely plugged into the primary mission God gave us. We put it this way: There is no CO-missioning without SUB-mission to the primary mission."* [2]

Bill goes on to explain what the primary mission God gave us is:

> *"He commissioned you to demonstrate the will of God, "on earth as it is in Heaven," transforming this planet into a place radiant and saturated with His power and presence.'* [3]

In other words our mission is to expand the Kingdom of God and bring Heaven to earth.

We are to be committed to the mission He gave us, but let us remember we have all that we need, but more than that, He partners with us in that mission.

We also read John's gospel:

> *"You did not choose me, but I chose you and appointed you to go and bear fruit - fruit that will last. …"*
>
> *John 15:16*

We read that part of our demonstration of the Kingdom of God is to bear fruit. Just as Christ is the exact representation of the Father so we also are to represent God. As we saw in chapter five 'In His Image' we have His nature inside of us, and

---

[2] Johnson, B., (2005) *The Supernatural Power of a Transformed Mind.* Destiny Image. p.38 (Permission granted)
[3] Johnson, B., (2005) *The Supernatural Power of a Transformed Mind.* Destiny Image. p.38 (Permission granted)

so when people see us they see the Father. We are representing the Father to those around us. We are to reveal the very nature of who He is, we are to bring the Kingdom to earth, we are to be Jesus' hands and feet. As we reveal the love that He has, they see the goodness of who He is. We are carriers of God.

If this is true then we need to understand something. Since He cannot dwell where there is impurity, it also follows that we are pure, that we are holy and blameless.

"For He chose us in Him before the creation of the world to be holy and blameless in His sight."

Ephesians 1:4

We have been chosen by Him to partner with Him to reveal His nature and character to the world; how can we do that if we are not holy and blameless? He has made us holy. He no longer sees us as we were, unlike a piece of fruit you put back because it is bruised or damaged, He does not see that, He sees us as His chosen ones, His special people whom He loves.

Look at what the psalmist writes:

"Know that the Lord has set apart the godly for Himself; the Lord will hear when I call to Him."

Psalm 4:3

We have been set apart and chosen, we are distinct from the world. As we saw earlier we have been chosen and because of that when we call He hears us:

"This is the confidence we have approaching God: that if we ask anything according to His will, He hears us. And if we know that He hears us – whatever we ask – we know that we have what we asked of Him."

1 John 5:14-15

If our purpose is to partner with Him, then we have all that is required to do it. Everything we need to partner with Him is at our disposal; there is nothing more we need. Just as a partner of a business is aware of the entire workings of the business, they have access to every area of the business, so too do we. We have an all areas access pass to Heaven. We have access to everything we need. As partners with Him, we have everything we need to succeed.

Let's go back to the example of the sports team. Once the match is underway, those that were picked last may have an excuse to play badly; after all the ability they have is less than another person. However, on flip side, if you are one of the first to be picked it is because you have shown you have a skill in that area; your ability is such that you can be relied upon. When you play well you are thanked by your team mates for the effort you put in. Even if you have an off day, it is recognised that you still have all that it takes, you would still be one of the first to be picked next time. Having been chosen by Him to partner with Him for His mission, we can all have an off day, we still sin and make mistakes. However, the Holy Spirit who lives inside us never has an off day, there is never a time that He does not perform at His best, therefore although we may feel as though we have messed up, in Him we have not.

We were chosen before the creation of the world (Ephesians 1:4). Paul writes to the church in Thessalonica:

> *"But we ought always to thank God for you, brothers loved by the Lord, because from the beginning God chose you to be saved through the sanctifying work of the Holy Spirit and through belief in the truth."*
>
> *2 Thessalonians 2:13*

Even if we think we have had off day, Heaven recognises that we are chosen and loved by Him.

Elsewhere we read:

> *"The LORD your God is with you, the Mighty Warrior who saves. He will take great delight in you; in His love he will no longer rebuke you, but will rejoice over you with singing."*
>
> *Zephaniah 3:17*

The idea of rejoicing is to celebrate, we are championed by Him. He is for us. So we can see that we are chosen and He celebrates us. That is how much He thinks of us.

I shared this story before, but I feel it is worth repeating: One morning I was driving to work, and I asked the Father "What do you expect of me today?" I was astounded by His response, "I don't expect anything of my children." It was quite early on in my journey into sonship and so I replied "What do you mean you don't expect anything of your children?" His response blew me away, with love He spoke these words "If I expect something of you that would give you the ability to fail, my children never fail me." What freeing words from a loving Father. We are chosen by Him because He loves us, because He wants us to partner with Him, but to partner in such a way that we cannot fail. As we read in chapter five 'In His Image', we saw that we are to represent Him, by being in relationship with Him, in other words in partnership with Him.

We have seen that in this partnership with the Father to which we are called, not only that but also we are celebrated by Him. We saw in chapter seven 'Adopted', that as His adopted sons we are given a new name, so therefore, we are invited to carry the name that is above all other names, the name of Jesus (Philippians 2:9). So you see, if we are chosen and we carry the name of Jesus, we really cannot fail.

Just as when my wife married me, she took on a new name, she was no longer known by her maiden name. From that moment she was known by my family name. We now take on a new name; we are now called according to Paul in the book of Romans:

"...sons of the living God."

Romans 9:26 [4]

As we have been chosen we have also become partners with Him, we are chosen as partners to the family business 'Father and Sons'. Within that partnership we are called by a new name, 'sons' and therefore if we are sons in the family business, with the Father ultimately in charge, it is impossible for us to fail.

What a great privilege to be chosen by Him, we have become His inheritance with such value and worth, that we are seen as His special people. We are chosen to partner with Him in the mission of Heaven.

---

[4] This whole section in Romans 9:25-26 is taken from the book of Hosea. See specifically Hosea 1:10 and Hosea 2:23. We see clearly here, that we have been called despite anything we have done or even deserved.

Prayer:

Father, I thank You that You have chosen me. You have selected me to partner with You because You love me. Father I thank You that You see me as Your special one, Your right hand man. No matter how I see myself, in You I have worth, help me to see myself as You see me. I believe the truth that I am worthy, I have value, I have been chosen because you think I am the best. Thank You that because of You I cannot fail and I have everything I need at my disposal.

The Apple of His Eye

A dictionary definition of the phrase 'The apple of His eye' means "the particular object of a person's affection or regard; a greatly cherished person."

What a beautiful description. To be the apple of His eye means we are the object of God's affection; we are cherished by Him. Have you ever stopped to reflect on what it means to be the object of His affection? I think part of this is that His focus is completely towards us. It is like everything else is blurred, all He can focus on is you. There is nothing that will distract Him from looking on you or me. Just as a mother looks upon her new-born child, all she can see is the beautiful baby she and the father created. There is such joy, there is such pleasure and there is nothing that will stop her from looking at this new creation. She looks upon her child with love and pride. The new mother looks upon her child to savour every movement her baby makes. She does not want to miss anything.

We have His full attention. He does not for one minute glance away from us or turn His face from us. His love is so great that

He cannot do anything apart from give you His full attention. In the book of Hebrews we read:

"… God has said, "Never will I leave you; never will I forsake you."

Hebrews 13:5

Also, in Numbers we read:

"The Lord bless you and keep you; the Lord make His face shine upon you and be gracious to you; the Lord turn His face toward you and give you His peace."

Numbers 6:24-26

What an amazing promise we have from the Father. Firstly, He will never leave us. Not just that, He turns His face towards us. He has such a great love for each of His beloved children that He turns His face towards us. It is a deliberate act. It is an act that says I choose to turn toward you, but more than that, I gaze upon you completely, so much so that we can receive His peace in that simple act. All we have to do is acknowledge and recognise that His face is turned towards us.

When you are talking face to face with someone, do you feel like you have their full attention? Do you feel like they are taking an interest in what you are saying? If they keep looking away, do they seem to be more distracted? I guess the answer is clear. You see, we have His full attention. He is never distracted by something or someone else. He turns His face towards you and He is in effect saying I am taking complete and total interest in you. Father God has so much love for us that whatever we do, whatever we say to Him, He is always wholeheartedly interested in us. He is never distracted by anything else. Just as when my wife talks to me, I want to show her that I am totally interested in all that she has to say, I give her my full attention and consequently she feels valued and loved. But the reverse is also true if, I fail to give her my full attention or I appear to be distracted, she would question me and not feel so valued and loved.

Because of Jesus and the immense love He has for each of us, we can be confident that we will have His full attention all of the time. He is never distracted, and so we never have to feel as though we are not valued or loved by Him. It is because of Jesus that we are the apple of the Father's eye.

I remember the day I got married; I was standing at the alter waiting for my bride to walk down the aisle. At this point I could only imagine the vision of beauty that would soon come walking towards me from the other end of the church. Then it happened; I glimpsed movement; I was able to see, my previous imaginings were now a reality. As my bride walked down the aisle, all I looked at was her, all I wanted to see was her. At that moment it was like there was nobody else in the room, it felt like it was just my bride and I. All our friends and family that had come to celebrate with us were no longer part of my view; I was totally focused on the beauty that was walking towards me. At that moment it was like time stood still, all I could see was her, all I wanted to see was her, nothing else mattered. I watched her as she continued to move towards me, I did not want to miss anything. I watched as she came closer, I saw the sparkle in her eyes as our eyes met; I saw the smile appear on her face. I saw the love she had and I could see the joy she was experiencing. This is the same picture we have with Father God, He is totally focused on you and I, it is as though there is no one else around. He notices every detail in our lives, nothing misses His attention.

As we shall see later, the meaning of the phrase "the apple of His eye" is a reference to the tiny reflection you see of yourself in another person's pupil.

For many years I heard the phrase "we are the apple of God's eye" but did not really understand it. I thought it was a nice idea, it sounded like a good thing, but what does it really mean? How is it related to being made in His image?

There are four times the phrase appears in the Bible, I want to take time to look at each passage separately:

"Keep me as the apple of Your eye; hide me in the shadow of Your wings."

Psalm 17:8

This is a prayer of protection. We can see here a picture of delicacy of the eye. The psalmist understands this, and he understands how vulnerable the eye is. However, he also understands how important the eye is.

We are important to God. We are vulnerable, even though at times we may have either thought or said "I can do this", or "I can overcome", "I don't need help". We are conditioned by society to think that we are to be strong; that we are the masters of our own destiny. However, I am also sure many of us have also thought 'I cannot do this; it is too hard, if only someone would come to my aid, I want to be strong, I need to be strong, but I feel so weak I just cannot.' This second thought suggests that maybe we do have vulnerability. We all need other people and we all need to feel safe and secure. God is our source of comfort, God is our source of strength, God is our source of protection. He knows just how much we need His comfort, His strength and His protection. We were not designed to be independent, we were created to be in relationship; both in relationship with others, but more importantly with Father God.

Think about that new-born baby again, where the mother is focused so much on it, what mother would not protect that little defenceless, vulnerable child? So too our Father in Heaven is just the same. He would go to any length to protect us. He has gone to any length, He sent His Son to die on a cross, to die in our place.

This verse suggests we are very valuable to God, so much so that He would automatically protect us just as you or I would react if there was potential harm to the apple (pupil) of our eye.

Who can endure being stabbed in the eye? This is the type of pain He feels when any harm comes to us. This is just an immense love, the Father loves us with such a great love that He does not want any harm to come to us, He will do anything to protect us from such a thing. I can appreciate that type of love. If someone was attacking me and trying to poke me in the eye, I'm sure I would protect my eye to the best of my ability, in fact it would be a natural response, a response that would require no thought, it would be an instinctive reaction.

The protection that the Father gives us, is just as instinctive, it is a natural response of a good loving Father, there is no thought required. He does not stop to watch to see if we can overcome it ourselves. He comes to our rescue without a moment of hesitation, without a second thought.

There is nothing that holds the Father's love from us, there is nothing on the same basis that would not stop His protection coming towards us.

Let us look at the second passage:

> *"For this is what the Lord Almighty says: "After he has honoured Me and has sent Me against the nations that have plundered you – for whoever touches you touches the apple of His eye."*
>
> *Zechariah 2:8*

What a beautiful picture! There is so much protection and care given by God, if anyone so much as tries to harm us, it is like God Himself is being harmed. Who does not try to protect themselves from harm? As we are made in His image, we are His children and so He does all He can to protect His own, because it is as if He Himself is being attacked.

I remember one evening I was driving home and approaching a large and busy roundabout and I felt God say "stop" even though the lights gave me right of way. I stopped and someone jumped the lights at pace and had I not responded to His prompting, I would have been seriously injured or worse.

I am reminded of Job:

> *"Does Job fear God for nothing?" Satan replied. "Have You not put a hedge of protection around him and his household and everything he has?"*
>
> *Job 1:9-10*

Job was protected by God and so are we. Satan understood this; he understood that he was not allowed to harm Job. It was as if no matter what tried to come against Job, there was a much stronger force of protection which could withstand anything that was coming towards him. Just a few verses later we read:

> *"The LORD said to satan, "Very well, then, everything he has is in your hands, but on the man himself do not lay a finger."*
>
> *Job 1:12*

You might read this and be thinking that God removed His protection, but notice God says satan is not allowed to lay a finger on Job. Still Job was being protected by God. There were limits to the harm satan was allowed to bring to Job, and even then, he had to ask permission of God.

If ever you question how much God protects you remind yourself that we are just like Job. We are created in the same way that Job was created, we are loved in the same way that he was loved; therefore, satan has the same restrictions over us as he did with Job. The protection that was afforded to Job is also afforded to us.

You may be thinking, hold on, Job was the most righteous man (Job 1:1, 8) I am not like him. Wrong! We are just like him. Because of Jesus, we are made righteous.

> *"This righteousness from God comes through faith in Jesus Christ to all who believe."*
>
> *Romans 3:22*

When the Father looks at us He sees us as righteous, He sees we are His children. He loves us with such an amazing love that there is no distinction between us and Job, therefore the protection Job had is the same protection we have. We are protected by Father God and therefore just as Job appeared to have an impenetrable shield, so too do we. We have the constant, ever strong arms of a loving Father holding us and protecting us.

Within the first two passages we have looked at, it seems as though this thought of being the apple of God's eye is about protection. Let us to continue and look at the third passage:

"In a desert land he found him, in a barren and howling waste. He shielded him and cared for him; he guarded him as the apple of His eye…"

Deuteronomy 32:10

I think this verse speaks of tenderness, of a deep longing, a desire that He has for each of us because the Lord treasures His people. He loves us so much, words cannot express, and our minds cannot fully comprehend such a great love. This verse suggests that He will do anything to guard us. The meaning is that being in the apple of His eye is to be in His very pupil, so great is His love for us, that just as we would protect our own eyes, so He will protect us.

The fourth passage is found in Proverbs:

"Keep my commands and you will live; guard my teachings as the apple of your eye"

Proverbs 7:2

This final passage is slightly different, instead of being told we are the apple of His eye, we are exhorted to love God's word, to keep His word at the centre of our hearts. Why? As we hold the teaching of His word close to us, then it becomes a lamp to our feet and a light to our path (Psalm 119:105). Simply, I think this continues to speak of His protection over us, His love over us. God is saying that if we keep our focus on His word then that too will protect us. Look at Psalm 119:

"I have hidden Your word in my heart that I might not sin against You."

Psalm 119:11

If our focus is on His word, on His love letter to us, then that in itself protects us; not necessarily a physical protection, but a spiritual one; His word helps us not to sin. He has given us His word that we may be protected from sin.

To be the apple of His eye is to know and experience His protection and the security that brings us. If for one moment He turned His face away, if He stopped looking at us, how could we be sure of his protection for us? His love for us is so tender that He does all He can to bring us protection, He does not want to see harm come to us.

In all verses, the meaning is the same; it is the sense of protection because of His love for us. We have seen it is like He looks at us so closely that He sees Himself in us. He sees Himself in us because we were created in His image. Therefore, when He looks at us He sees a reflection of Himself. What a thought! When the Father looks at you and I He sees Himself, with that in mind why would He not want to protect us? If someone was intending to harm us, to Him it would be as though someone was bringing Him harm. The reverse is also true; if we were to look into His eyes we would literally see our reflection in Him.

We have seen that to be the apple of God's eye is likened to being the pupil or the very centre of His focus. Could we say we are the centre of His attention? He loves us so much, with such abundance, with such adoration; He looks upon us with joy and love, so much so that He cannot take His eyes from us. His love is so great that He will do anything to protect us; He protects us as He would if someone was trying to poke His eye out, with fervent passion! Without a second thought, He sees us as vulnerable; as a new-born baby is loved and vulnerable, so we are to Him.

However, we might have times in our lives where the outcome feels different, and it seems difficult to marry up Father's heart to protect us with our own experiences. We live in a fallen and broken world and we have free will. As a result we will get hurt by others, either intentionally or otherwise. God's promise of protection does not include assurance that we will not suffer pain or loss.

"I have told you these things, so that in me you may have peace. In this world you will have trouble. But take heart! I have overcome the world"

John 16:33

We live in a world where we experience the reality of an enemy, the devil, and his kingdom of darkness; in 1 John we are reminded that this world is under the enemy's control:

"We know that we are children of God, and that the whole world is under control of the evil one."

1 John 5:19

We see the consequences of this both in the world at large but also I'm sure in our own lives at times. When we experience situations like this I would encourage you to ask Jesus 'show me where you were when this happened?' or 'Jesus, how did you feel about that situation?' and listen to His response.

My wife and I have led people through Sozo sessions who have experienced abuse and they would legitimately be able to ask 'where was God's protection then?' Where was God when I most needed Him? Why did He not stop that happening? I remember one such Sozo, and the lady being ministered to heard the Father say to her that He was there with her the entire time and His protection was still upon her. The lady received complete freedom knowing it was not the will of the Father for that to happen, and she was able to be restored knowing the protection and love of the Father, and that He was also grieved by what happened.[1]

Treasured Possession.

In the third passage we read that we are treasure to Him, so what does this mean? How does this have an impact on us?

As I am sure you are aware a king or queen has many treasures, these treasures are very valuable. In the United Kingdom the Tower of London has special rooms dedicated solely for the crown jewels. As you can imagine there is tight security surrounding them. If they were not of value, the security would not be needed.

We are valuable to Him, we are His treasure. Let us read three passages in Deuteronomy to explore this more:

> *"for you are a people holy to the Lord your God. Out of all the peoples on the face of the earth, the Lord has chosen you to be His treasured possession."*
>
> *Deuteronomy 14:2*

---

[1] If you have experienced a similar trauma I would encourage you to a have a Sozo session. Please visit https://www.bethelsozo.org.uk/ to find your nearest Sozo Team in the UK.

> *"And the Lord has declared this day that you are His people, His treasured possession as He promised, and that you are to keep His commands."*
>
> *Deuteronomy 26:18*

Notice He chose us to be His treasured possession. We belong to Him; we are of immense value and worth to Him. This is true whether we believe it or not.

Finally, if we look at the third passage:

> *"For you are a people holy to the Lord your God. The Lord your God has chosen you out of all the peoples on the face of the earth to be His people, His treasured possession. The Lord did not set His affection on you and choose you because you were more numerous than the other peoples, for you were the fewest of all peoples. But it was because the Lord loved you…"*
>
> *Deuteronomy 7:6-8a*

Our background and our abilities have no influence on this fact. Whether you feel worthless or you feel you have no value or significance, we can see clearly that the Lord chose us. He chose us because of Him and not because of who we are. The truth remains; we *are* His treasured possession. We have so much worth to Him, we have so much value in His sight that the very best security He has is surrounding and protecting us. His very face is turned towards us.

To be the apple of God's eye means that He cherishes us. The value He places upon you and I is immeasurable; we are like a treasure chest full of priceless jewels to Him. We are so valuable to Him that there are no lengths He will not go to, to protect us. We are His prized possession; we are the object of

His desire. He looks on us with such a deep longing, a deep desire, He can never remove His gaze from us. The instant any harm may be coming to us, He is there to guard us, watching over us and keeping us safe.

To be made in the image of God demonstrates a love that we cannot comprehend. The more revelation I have of His love for me the more I experience this love, then the more I realise there is to experience! Being the apple of the Father's eye is a wonderful picture of this love, it is a beautiful picture of the depth of His love for us.

I pray that each of us grows in this amazing revelation of the depth of love He has for us; that we begin to grasp truly what it means to be the apple of His eye. Picture if you will the Father looking at you so intently, so deeply that His whole focus is on you. He is looking at you with such pride that there is nothing that will distract Him from looking at you. He is looking at you so intensely, that if you were to lock eyes with His you would see your reflection in His eyes. As you do, look deeper into His eyes and notice the love He has for you, notice His joy as He looks upon you, notice how tenderly His eyes look as He looks at you. See that He cannot remove His focus from you. You and only you are the object of His love. He is looking at you so profoundly and so closely that He sees himself in you, He sees the love He has for you, and He sees the goodness He has in you. He sees that all of Him is in you.

Prayer:

Father I thank You that I am the apple of Your eye. Give me a greater revelation of what that really means for me because I want to experience more of the love You have for me. I want a deeper revelation of how You *see me, I know if I understand more of how You see me then I will desire more of You. Thank You that I **am** Your treasured possession, that to You I have so much worth and value and You see me like a priceless jewel. Thank You that You protect me, shield me and You watch over me.*

Mark Russell

Royalty

Have you ever wondered what it would be like to be a member of a royal family? What about from their perspective? What must it be like to grow up in a family that appears to have it all? They have many privileges; several houses and palaces, the authority that the name carries and the respect they are given because of who they are. Being a member of a royal family means they have duties to perform; each member, whether Queen or Prince and Princess, each represent the royal family, they are representatives for the royal family. When they speak, it is expected that they are speaking on behalf of that family. They are in effect ambassadors of the monarchy.

I have come to realise that we are born into such a family. When a royal baby is born he or she is automatically part of the royal household. That baby is a prince or princess by birthright and they have no choice in the matter. So too are we; by birthright we are born into the royal household of God. We have become royalty and we are ambassadors for the Kingdom of Heaven.

Let's take a look at 1 Peter:

*'But **you are** a chosen people, a **royal** priesthood, a holy nation, a people belonging to God, that you may declare the praises of Him who called you out of darkness into His wonderful light. Once **you were not** a people, but **now you are** the people of God; once **you had not** received mercy, but **now you have** received mercy'*

1 Peter 2:9-10 (emphasis added)

Firstly, note that the passage is in the present tense. Peter goes to great lengths to point out what we were not and by comparison what we now are. 'Once you were not' compared with the phrase 'but now you are' clearly demonstrates that who we are now is different to who we were. Peter seems to repeat this idea with the phrase 'once you had not' compared with 'but now you have'. Peter does not want there to be any mistake; the two phrases 'you were not' and 'you had not' are both past tense, whilst the phrases 'now you are' and 'now you have' are both present tense. This is not a passage that suggests this is something for us in the future. We have already made the transition from one to the other. We are the people of God, we have received mercy. Peter is making these claims as he is writing to believers. Therefore, this passage in Peter is true now for anyone who believes in Jesus.

Notice also before the comparison we are told 'you are a chosen people, a royal priesthood, a holy nation, a people belonging to God.' This is not something we can look forward to in Heaven, this is not something we have to attain. It is not something that we might hope to be by following certain criteria, it is something that we *are*. Jesus is the one who makes us royal, we have been chosen, He is the one who has made us holy. We have not accomplished this on our own merit, nor is it something we have achieved. Jesus has bought us. It is our birth right. When we were born again we became the people of God. We have now received mercy and being royal is simply part of who we are as a child of God. It is our God given identity.

What does it mean to be a royal priesthood? Firstly we need to understand what it means to be a priest.

As the chosen people of God we have full and complete access to Him, unlike the priests of old who could only enter after ceremonial washings, presenting themselves with the blood of goats and lambs. The priest was the one who represented the ordinary people before God, he was the one who came before God on behalf of God's people.

'But only the high priest entered the inner room, and that only once a year, and never without blood, which he offered for himself and for the sins the people had committed in ignorance.'

Hebrews 9:7

However, with the death and resurrection of Jesus everything changed.

'Then the curtain of the temple was torn in two from top to bottom'

Mark 15:38

It was the veil that divided us; it was the veil that kept the people, who were sinners and therefore unclean, separate from the Holy God. If anyone entered through the curtain who was unclean, even the priest, if he had not made himself ceremonially clean would die. We are now the priesthood. We can come before Him. We have complete and total access; there are no restrictions. Once He was unapproachable, but now He is approachable because the veil has been torn. It was torn from top to bottom. This was not something that man had done; in fact it was almost impossible for man to break it. Only God was able to tear down the veil, it is only God who has made it possible for us to come freely into His presence.

Since the veil has now been torn in two, there is now no longer any separation between us and Father God. We now have complete access to the Holy Place; we have access to the Father:

'Therefore brothers, since we have confidence to enter the Most Holy Place by the blood of Jesus, by a new and living way opened up for us through the curtain, that is, His body, and since we have a great priest over the house of God, let us draw near to God with a sincere heart in full assurance of faith...'

Hebrews 10:19-22

'For through Him we both have access to the Father by one Spirit.'

Ephesians 2:18

It was the priests of the Old Testament that represented the people of Israel to God. Now we are that priest, we are the ones who have access to Heaven. We are the ones who can come before the Father, we are the people who represent God to those around us. It was the priest that served the people, it was they who worshipped. But we are now the ones who can worship Him, we are the ones who can proclaim His goodness through what we do and what we say.

So, why are we royal? It is worth noting that the priests have a kingly rank; they are only subject to God and Christ. The book of Hebrews teaches that Melchizedek was both king & priest, and Jesus was both king and priest in the order of Melchizedek (Hebrews 6:20-7:1) Christ is the King of Kings and as kings have kingdoms, we now serve Him in His kingdom. We function within and from that kingdom. When a king or queen dies the next person in line to the throne is the prince. We are now adopted as children of God; therefore we are of royal descent.

Through our adoption into the family of God we become part of the Father's family. This gives us the same rights as Jesus, so much so that we are called His brothers:

'Both the one who makes men holy and those who are made holy are of the same family. So Jesus is not ashamed to call them brothers.'

Hebrews 2:11

We are now of the same family as Jesus, more than that we are His brothers, as Jesus is Prince of Peace, we too are princes in the Kingdom of God.

If we truly are made in the image of God, we are made in the image of a King.

We saw earlier that a member of the royal household has responsibilities, they serve the kingdom and they are ambassadors for that kingdom. We serve the Kingdom of God, we speak for His domain and we should be declaring the goodness of that kingdom. As servants of the Heavenly royal household we should be proclaiming the truths of the kingdom of God in which we serve and demonstrate the nature of that Kingdom. Our words and our actions represent the Him.

We may need to change the way we think in order to fully understand and appreciate our own royalty. If we understand our royal identity then our mind-set, how we think of ourselves, how we see ourselves and indeed how we treat ourselves, needs to change and come into line with how the King sees us. Royal people know who they are. Royal people both think and know they are royalty. Consequently they conduct themselves as though they are royalty, in a regal manner. True royal figures respect others and consider them in a similar way. R Puttman says:

> *"Royalty is a revelation that is focused on our values. It is learning to love ourselves the way that God loves us. As we learn to value ourselves, we reflect that same value back towards others. If we don't value ourselves, we don't value others as well."* [1]

A few years ago as I was beginning to learn about being royalty in the household of God, I was thinking about healing and praying for the sick. I sensed the Father begin to speak to me, He said "When a prince speaks he expects to be obeyed, he expects the very thing he has asked to be done, will be done. So too should you expect to see healing, you should expect the kingdom of this world, which is a lower kingdom, to submit to the authority of the Kingdom of Heaven."

---

[1] Puttman, R. (2013) *School of Kingdom Ministry Manual*, Coaching Saints Publications. p.121. (Permission granted)

I began to understand a little of the authority the prince or any member of a royal household has. I began to realise that when we pray for the sick on the same basis should expect sickness to flee. We are part of the Heavenly royal family with the same authority, so when we tell sicknesses to go, we should expect that sickness to obey.

I am still seeking to understand why this does not always happen, why when we pray for the sick the sickness sometimes remains. I remember a time when I was praying for someone to be healed, and as I was praying Father showed me something else that He wanted to do with their heart. As I asked the person about this they began to cry. As I prayed into this revelation from the Father the person was more touched by that than if they had been physically healed. Of course whether the person is healed or not, it is important that they feel loved by Him. There have been many who have sought to bring clarity to such an experience. All I am convinced of is who I am and the authority I have as a child of God, as a member of the royal household of Heaven. Therefore such a discrepancy should cause me to continue to seek Him further, to press deeper and not make up a theological explanation, no matter how good the justification may or may not be that could ultimately lead me to not expect healing when I pray for the sick.

Jesus says:

> *'But seek first His kingdom, and His righteousness and all these things will be given to you has well'.*
>
> *Matthew 6:33*

It is quite clear, seek Him, seek His presence and His Kingdom first.

I think our first and foremost calling is to seek Him. We are to seek the face of the giver and not the hand of the giver. When we seek the face, a by-product is that we receive the gifts. I have heard people say: "Why do we need miracles, why can't we just have Him, isn't He enough?" Whilst it may be true that He is enough, I believe it is impossible to have Him without the miracles. It is impossible to have Him without change, it is impossible to have just Him and nothing of His nature or character also.

If we seek Him and His kingdom first then something follows; His presence. With His presence comes the manifestation of His Kingdom. When we have the manifestation of His Kingdom then in turn we have miracles. If a kingdom rules, then it stands to reason that it should reign too. Therefore, if a kingdom rules and reigns then the ideology of that ruling kingdom will be established. It is expected that the reigning kingdom will also have its rules obeyed. The Kingdom of God reigns and therefore when it comes against something that is not of that kingdom, the lesser kingdom will bow the knee to the greater. So, if we seek Him and His Kingdom, we should expect to see healing, we should expect sickness to bow the knee, we should expect to see those with any kind of sickness made well.

As we are members of the royal household of God, as we are priests in the Kingdom and as priests we continue to proclaim the Kingdom, it follows therefore that it should also be true that we see sicknesses flee.

As we are priests and are now seen as royalty, it is our role to bring out the royalty in other people. We are to dress them in royal robes, just as the Old Testament priest had specific garments (Exodus 39), we too as royal priests wear royal garments. We are to encourage others to continue to wear such garments. We are called to bring out the best in people. Kris Vallotton in his book 'Supernatural Ways of Royalty' addresses this in a way that I hope will bring further clarity.

"As the Royal Priesthood of God, we are called to develop a culture in our homes, churches, businesses and ultimately in nations that brings out the best in individuals, facilitating their princely destinies. We do this by seeing and treating others as ourselves not as we are, but as God created us to be. This knowledge and love can only come out of intimacy with God. No longer are we His slaves, but His friends, walking by His side as kings and queens of the court." [2]

Our role as priests then, is to help people to see their true identity as royal children of God.

Saint versus Sinner

I mentioned earlier that the veil kept the sinner separate from the Holy God, but we know that the veil no longer exists. What does this mean? We are now saints and we are no longer seen as sinners. The moment we repented and gave our life to Jesus, our identity transformed from being a sinner to being a saint. When Paul writes his letters he often writes to 'the saints'

---

[2] Johnson, B. and Vallotton, K. (2006) *The Supernatural Ways of Royalty: Discovering Your Rights and Privileges of Being a Son or Daughter of God.* Destiny Image. p.89. (Permission granted)

> *'... To the church of God in Corinth, together will all the saints throughout Achaia'*
>
> *2 Corinthians 1:1*
>
> *'... To the saints in Ephesus, the faithful in Christ Jesus:'*
>
> *Ephesians 1:1*
>
> *'... To all the saints in Christ Jesus who are in Philippi, together with the bishops and deacons:'*
>
> *Philippians 1:1 (KJV)*

Paul is writing to different churches, he is writing to those who are in Christ Jesus. Notice Paul does not say "To the sinners in Christ", he refers to those in Christ as saints.

Part of being of royal descent and a member of God's royal household is that we are saints and no longer sinners.

According to Catholic tradition a person can only become a saint five years after the person's death. Their life has to be scrutinised, various tests passed and they need to be deemed to have led a holy life in obedience to God's will.

Whilst I do not hold to catholic tradition I want to look at some of these rules; you will see that every Christian, that includes you and me, in Christ have met these standards.

Firstly the person must have died. As we look at the next two scriptures you will notice that we have all met this standard.

> *'For we know that our old self was crucified with Him so that the body of sin might be done away with, that we should no longer be slaves to sin –*

because anyone who has died has been freed from sin. Now if we died with Christ, we believe that we will also live with Him.'

Romans 6:6-8

'I have been crucified with Christ and I no longer live, but Christ lives in me.'

Galatians 2:20

Paul clearly teaches that we have died with Christ, our old way of life has passed away and we have become a new creation (2 Corinthians 5:17). Therefore if the first test to being saints is to die, we have all done that. Notice too, we have died to sin; sin should no longer be a part of who we are. Certainly the Father does not see us that way, He does not see the sin that was part of our old life, He sees us as we are, purified.

This leads us to the second test.

Let us now look at the second test. We are to have led a holy life. What does the bible say?

'And by that will we have been made holy through the sacrifice of the body of Jesus Christ once for all.'

Hebrews 10:10

We have been made holy. Jesus makes us holy by His blood. Paul also teaches that because of Jesus we are made holy:

'It is because of Him that you are in Christ Jesus, who has become for us wisdom from God – that is, our righteousness, holiness and redemption.'

1 Corinthians 1:30

It is because of Jesus that we are made holy, we cannot be holy in and of ourselves in the true sense of the word. There is no person who is able to meet up to that standard, not even a proven catholic saint. Yet God says:

'Be holy because I am holy.'

1 Peter 1:16

Jesus is the one who has made us holy through sanctification. It is because of Jesus' blood that not only does God not see our sin, but much more than that, He sees us as holy.

In the true sense of the catholic test, we pass the major two tests for sainthood.

It is impossible by definition to be both a sinner and a saint, we are one or the other. It seems clear because we have seen Paul refers to the churches as saints and never as sinners. A saint is someone who is in Christ, that same someone is also holy. Paul's first greeting to the Corinthian church expresses this:

*'To the church of God in Corinth, to those **sanctified** in Christ Jesus and called to be **holy**, together with all those everywhere who call on the name of the Lord Jesus Christ – their Lord and ours:'*

1 Corinthians 1:2 (emphasis added)

Notice the words sanctified and holy. To be sanctified means to be purified or consecrated to God. To be holy also has that same thought. The original Greek word translated sanctify *(hagiazō)* comes from the root word to be a saint. Therefore we can clearly understand that to be sanctified and to be holy, is to be a saint. A holy person is a saint and if the holy person is a saint, how then can he be a sinner? Or as Kris Vallotton suggests:

"If we believe we are sinners we will continue to sin" [3]

We need to change the way we think. We need to start believing that we are saints and not sinners. If we think we are sinners we are more likely to sin or assume we will sin, as we believe that is our identity. Being a royal priesthood and a member of God's royal household means we are saints. We have been given a new identity, we are now saints. The old identity of being a sinner is no longer a valid one, it is not who we are. Just as a child of royalty has the title prince or princess, so too we have the title saint. When someone marries into the royal household they are given a title, they are given a new name. The old name they possessed is no longer theirs, they are called by the new name. We have been given a new name; we have been given such a title. We are now called saints of God; we are now called a royal priesthood. As we saw in the chapter Co-heirs with God, a name holds meaning. We no longer hold the original name, we no longer have the identity that the old name brought us, and people should not call us by that name. We have a new identity, a royal identity.

Members of royalty know they are intended to do great things. Some will one day rule a nation, however no matter where they are in line to the throne, they are expected to have great value to those around them. All members of royalty know they are

---

[3] Vallotton, K. (2016) *Kris Vallotton*. Available at: http://krisvallotton.com/we-are-not-sinners-we-are-saints/ (Accessed: 28th March 2020). (Permission granted) Read the entire blog for a better explanation of this idea of sinner verses saint.

important and will affect the lives of others, whether directly or indirectly.

It is time we walked in our new identity as saints, that we truly believed who Jesus has made us to be. I believe when we understand this with our hearts then we can begin to march forward with our head held high and we will carry ourselves as the royalty that we are. We will be able to value ourselves the way He values us. We can, therefore, affect other people's lives in a positive way and enable them to value themselves too. As a royal priesthood in the household of God, we act as saints and not sinners. As Kris Vallotton says:

> *"I want to encourage you to embrace your identity as a saint, repent from any partnership you've made with the lie that you're a sinner, and begin walking in the freedom that Jesus purchased for you! If this is a new revelation for you, I encourage you to declare this over yourself today: "I am a saint. I am a new creation. My natural tendency is to please God. I am free from the life of sin and shame! I bless my soul to be led by my spirit and Holy Spirit into all righteousness!"* [4]

Prayer:

> *Father, I recognise that because of Jesus I am a child of the King and by default that makes me a member of Your royal household. I am royalty. I choose to live in that truth and as I do this, reveal more of my royal heritage to me so that I might grow in understanding. I declare that I am no longer a sinner but a saint, and I choose today to live and walk in this truth.*

---

[4] Vallotton, K. (2019) *Kris Vallotton*. Available at: https://www.krisvallotton.com/believe-can-go-week-without-sinning (Accessed: 19th February 2022) (Permission granted)

Epilogue

Throughout this book my desire has been to explore who we really are in Christ; we have seen that who we are is because of the work of Jesus. I pray that as you have read each chapter you have received greater revelation from Father and consequently you are moving forward in your journey into living from a place of sonship. I encourage you to continually open your heart and grow in revelation, by seeking Him, asking Him and allowing Him to cause your head knowledge to become a life transforming heart revelation.

Jesus has set us free and therefore we are free indeed (John 8:36). When Jesus said "it is finished" (John 19:30) He meant everything! The Cross wasn't just about our salvation, the Cross also accomplished bringing us back into His family as sons and daughters and back to intimacy with Father. All the different themes contained within this book are completed in that one phrase of Jesus' on the cross.

My heart in writing this book is that as you have been reading it you have begun to see yourself as Father sees you. He sees you as His beloved son or daughter, a child in His family who has the right to call Him Abba Father. We have been chosen by Him and we are now adopted by Him.

We have been made in His image and therefore we are like Him. We can demonstrate His nature and character to others simply because we are like Him; because we have His Spirit living inside of us, or as John writes in his letter:

"As He is so we are in the world"

1 John 4:17 (NKJV)

Let's live in the truth that He desires intimacy with each one of us because of the incredible love He has for us. That same love is the reason we are His treasured possession. We are the apple of His eye and He goes to great lengths to protect each one of us. He gazes upon us with such loving intent; with a focus that is unwavering.

Our position as children of God is seated with Christ:

"He raised us up with Christ the exalted One, and we ascended with Him into the glorious perfection and authority of the heavenly realm, for we are now co-seated as one with Christ'"

Ephesians 2:6 (TPT)

We are seated with Christ in Heavenly places. We are royalty, we are brothers and sisters of the King of Kings, this is our identity and this is who we are. Our royalty is part of our inheritance, it has been freely given to us through Jesus, and our inheritance is a promise. Ultimately our inheritance is everything written about within the pages of this book.

Finally, I encourage all of us to keep pressing into Him to continually be transformed by the renewing of our mind, that we might gain even greater and deeper revelation of who we are, and that we are indeed made in His image. This book alone, without the Spirit of God, will remain as head knowledge. Only He can cause there to be a change within our hearts, and for our hearts to truly live as though we are made in His image.

About the Author

Mark is passionate about the church living from the revelation of God as their perfect loving Father and our identity as beloved children of God. Mark longs to see people receive inner healing and walk in the freedom of personal wholeness.

After graduating from Bible College, Mark has been involved in Christian ministry over the last 20 years including a number of years serving in Malawi. Mark and his wife are now based in beautiful East Devon and serve together in their home church, where they offer Bethel Sozo appointments (inner healing) and Father Heart Days and are looking at launching a School of Supernatural Life.

If you would like more information about Mark's ministry or want to get in touch, please head to his website: www.markandlaura.co.uk.

Printed in Great Britain
by Amazon